Veloce *Classic Reprint* Series

Montlhéry

The Story of the Paris Autodrome

A selection of Veloce publications –

Those were the days ... Series
Alpine Trials & Rallies 1910-1973 by Martin Pfundner
Brighton National Speed Trials by Tony Gardiner
Crystal Palace by S S Collins
Motor Racing at Brands Hatch in the Seventies by Chas Parker
Motor Racing at Goodwood in the Sixties by Tony Gardiner
Motor Racing at Oulton Park in the 60s by Peter McFadyen

Rally Giants Series
Ford Escort MkI by Graham Robson
Lancia Stratos by Graham Robson
Subaru Impreza by Graham Robson

General
1½-litre GP Racing 1961-1965 by Mark Whitelock
Alfa Tipo 33 by Ed McDonough and Peter Collins
Armstrong-Siddeley by Bill Smith
Bahamas Speed Weeks, The by Terry O'Neil
BMC Competitions Department Secrets by Stuart Turner, Marcus Chambers & Peter Browning
British 250cc Racing Motorcycles by Chris Pereira
British Cars, The Complete Catalogue of, 1895-1975 by Culshaw & Horrobin
BRM – a mechanic's tale by Richard Salmon
BRM V16 by Karl Ludvigsen
Coventry Climax Racing Engines by Des Hammill
Ford GT – Then and Now by Adrian Streather
Ford GT40 by Trevor Legate
GT – The World's Best GT Cars 1953-73 by Sam Dawson
Lola – The Illustrated History (1957-1977) by John Starkey
Lola – All The Sports Racing & Single-Seater Racing Cars 1978-1997 by John Starkey
Lola T70 – The Racing History & Individual Chassis Record 3rd Edition by John Starkey
Lotus 49 by Michael Oliver
Motor Racing – Reflections of a Lost Era by Anthony Carter
Motorsport in colour, 1950s by Martyn Wainwright
Porsche Racing by Brian Long
Porsche Rally History by Laurence Meredith
RAC Rally Action by Tony Gardiner
Redman, Jim – 6 times world motorcycle champion by Jim Redman
Unraced by Sam Collins
Works Minis, The last by Bryan Purves
Works Rally Mechanic by Brian Moylan

– visit www.veloce.co.uk to see our full range of exciting automotive books

First published in October 2006 by Veloce Publishing Limited, 33 Trinity Street, Dorchester DT1 1TT, England. Fax 01305 268864/e-mail info@veloce.co.uk/web www.veloce.co.uk or www.velocebooks.com
ISBN 13: 978-1-84584-052-5. ISBN 10: 1-84584-052-6. UPC 636847-04052-9.
Readers with ideas for automotive books, or books on other transport or related hobby subjects, are invited to write to the editorial director of Veloce Publishing at the above address.
British Library Cataloguing in Publication Data – A catalogue record for this book is available from the British Library.
Typesetting, design and page make-up all by Veloce Publishing Ltd on Apple Mac.
Printed by Replika Press in India.

Veloce *Classic Reprint* Series

Montlhéry

The Story of the Paris Autodrome

William 'Bill' Boddy M.B.E.

Foreword by Captain G. E. T. Eyston, O.B.E., M.C.

VELOCE PUBLISHING

THE PUBLISHER OF FINE AUTOMOTIVE BOOKS

Publisher's note

Veloce is proud to be able to reprint William 'Bill' Boddy's long out of print account of the life and times of the historically important Montlhéry race circuit.

First printed in 1961, the book has a style appropriate to the era, and one which we have altered as little as possible. The body text of the book is essentially unchanged, including tenses, to preserve its originality and sense of period. All of the photographic plates from the original book reappear in the reprint, although now placed more appropriately in relation to the chronology of the text: a few extra period images have been included too.

Most of the original photographs have been lost since 1961, so we have reproduced printed images to the best of our ability for this impression.

Lastly, this reprint does include an additional chapter briefly outlining what happened to the circuit after 1961.

Preface

I am sure that this book will unfold valuable knowledge of the sport we love, and make a fascinating addition to the library of every student of motoring history. It will shed light on a certain span of years crammed with motor racing and record-breaking which might now be classifed by some as pioneer days.

Notably, there were a great many attempts on international and world records on Montlhéry's speed track. Montlhéry was, of course, the ideal track for record-breaking: well-designed and constructed, with a reasonably smooth surface, and a short lap distance which made the task of spotting and control comparatively simple. Perhaps accomplishments in those early days were easier to finance because smaller crews were used; in fact, in many instances it was a case of 'do it yourself'.

The descriptions of the many great races make most entertaining reading, and I would like warmly to congratulate William Boddy on his fact-finding and accurate manner in which he has dealt with the events. The book is packed with thrilling accounts of the triumphs and disappointments on this historic ground.

Montlhéry is situated on a hill, and the ascent to the track from the main road used to be a testing ground for Citroën cars. Sometimes the surface was covered with a thin sheet of glassy ice. Traction on this was almost impossible. Once, with my companions, we were attempting to walk down this steep hill on a wintry day. To our amusement, the ferocious Alsatian from the local estaminet came rushing out to attack us. The dog struck the ice and went slithering on all fours out of sight down the incline.

It does not surprise me that mention is often made of adverse weather conditions, from strong winds to sheets of ice. I remember on one occasion being at the track with the Delage car, and spending days with a ladder on the high banking attacking the ice with picks.

Although Brooklands and Montlhéry are often described as places of uninterrupted full-throttle motoring, and this is substantially true, it could be mentioned that there was, at ultra-high speed, a regular method of 'getting round' which, if it was to be successful in not creating too much strain on the car, meant easing the throttle at the required moment before negotiating the turns. The thrill of it was to position the car correctly as it hit the high banking after leaving the straightaway.

Very many special cars are mentioned in the chapters which follow, but a particular one interested me: Constantini's roller-bearing 1500cc, straight-eight Bugatti, the actual car in which I subsequently won the Grand Prix de Boulogne.

For a considerable span of my early life, happy fate took me to Linas-Montlhéry at all times of the year: this is why I should be pardoned for occupying space in these pages. Although I like racing, record-breaking was in my blood, and it was by this means only that I could continue. Underlying all was a sheer love of the game and the ambition to promote something which might be useful to others. Somehow I think that this sentiment underlies the raison d'être of so many drivers in motor sport, and makes the taking of risks worthwhile.

The Montlhéry track with its road circuit exists today, and, ever since 1924, thanks to the initiative and sportsmanship of its original promoters, has performed an important role in the evolution of the motor car. History has been made on it, and all of us would like to express the hope that this Mecca of speed will long exist.

Shall I ever forget the occasion when there was that great chasm in the track? Or when the tip of the banking was illuminated with electric light bulbs, such as I used myself when the Hotchkiss successfully attacked the forty-eight hours world record? Memories will surely remain, and the lure of speed is such that I join with you in the enjoyment of the fascinating work which Mr Boddy has so successfully completed.

Capt George E T Eyston
OBE, MC, Legion d'Honneur

Contents

Introduction to this Classic Reprint

Although Montlhéry was fully active when the original edition of this book was written, sadly, it seemed even then that it was likely to follow Brooklands in closure. Now — so very regretfully — this has happened.

I am so pleased that Veloce, which has published much important motor racing history, has accepted my history of the seminal Parisian track and road-racing venues brought up to the time of its sad demise.

Bill Boddy, MBE
Llandrindod Wells
Wales

Original Introduction

This history of Montlhéry Autodrome is concerned with motor racing and record-breaking over a banked track, which is very different from high speed on a road circuit.

I have always been fascinated by pure uninterrupted full-throttle motoring, and this caused me to write about Brooklands (*The History of Brooklands Motor Course*: Grenville Publishing Co Ltd, 1957) the first motor course in the world where the curves were constructed as steep bankings so that it was unnecessary to 'lift one's foot' anywhere round the track.

Having compiled a record of activities at Brooklands, I was prompted by the advent of *The Veteran and Vintage Magazine* to look at similar activities which had taken place on that other banked motor course opened at Linas-Montlhéry in 1924. The articles I wrote dealt only with the vintage period, but Lord Montagu persuaded me to extend this Montlhéry story to the present day. This I have been glad to do because, whereas Brooklands motor course failed to survive the Second World War, and is now merely a collection of nostalgic memories and a memorial you see from the railway that flanks part of the grounds, Montlhéry track still flourishes, and you can go there and drive round on payment of a modest fee. I hope that this book will help those who do so to become familiar with the background of this fast course; to get to know the 'ghosts' of Montlhéry and their achievements.

Today, motor racing over banked tracks where speed is the prime motive is moribund except at Montlhéry and Monza.

Grand Prix cars, particularly the lightweight constructions of the present day, are unsuited to flat-out track racing, which is why the Monza organizers find it difficult to obtain entries for races round their new banked circuit, unless specialized cars (and drivers) can be attracted from America, where such racing still thrives, its culmination being the annual 500-mile race at Indianapolis where, although this is not a banked track at all, brakes are regarded as unnecessary and the lap record stands at no less than 149.6mph, in spite of the presence of four corners only slightly raised.

In this need for specialized cars lies, for me, the fascination of track racing. In the pages which follow you will fnd references to the long, lean, single-seater 'outer-circuit' racing cars which were typical of Brooklands and Montlhéry, particularly in the vintage era, for it was at these two tracks that full-bore racing was successfully carried on, the banked circuits at Sitges having but a very brief history. In later years all manner of cars – Grand Prix machines, sports cars, standard chassis with special bodywork, single-cylinder Formula 3 racers, and even family saloons – were to be seen speeding round the Montlhéry bankings, engaged in record-breaking onslaughts.

Indeed, it is with record-breaking that much of this book is concerned, so it behoves me to say something about it.

Records constitute the highest speed over a given distance

or greatest distance achieved by a car for a given duration, in a particular engine capacity class. Records have to be timed and observed by qualified officials of the national club in whose country the attempt is made, and these time-keepers and observers work to rules drawn up by the club's governing body in Paris, the CIA (formerly AIACR). They are required to ensure that distances are measured very accurately, and that the time-keeping arrangements and apparatus are above dispute. Short distance records have to be timed electrically by a tape machine or certified chronometers, these being actuated by a contact strip laid on the track, or by the passage of the car across a light beam acting on a photoelectric cell.

Very short distance records have to be run in opposite directions of the course, to cancel out the effects of wind and/or gradient. In recent years it has been necessary, in the case of the longer hand-timed records, to improve on a previous record by at least 1 per cent in order to overcome any minor errors in timing, while repairs can be made only at the car's depot on the track, and then only with spares and tools carried on the vehicle.

At the time when they were first introduced in 1904, the classes recognized were:

Class A: up to 1639cc
Class B: up to 2048cc
Class C: up to 2458cc
Class D: up to 2868cc
Class E: up to 3851cc
Class F: up to 4998cc
Class G: up to 7784cc
Class H: up to 13,929cc
Class J: over 13,929cc

World records, the fastest irrespective of class, are also recognized, and the distances ranged originally from the half-mile, kilometre and mile (which could be timed from a flying start) up to 1000 miles from a standing start, and from one hour up to twenty-four hours so far as duration records were concerned. The Brooklands authorities also recogized their own horsepower class records of 16hp, 21hp, 26hp, 40hp, 60hp and 90hp, RAC rating.

In 1925 the international classes were changed to those prevailing today, as follows:

Class H: not exceeding 750cc
Class G: over 750cc up to 1100cc
Class F: over 1100cc up to 1500cc
Class E: over 1500cc up to 2000cc
Class D: over 2000cc up to 3000cc
Class C: over 3000cc. up to 5000cc
Class B: over 5000cc up to 8000cc
Class A: over 8000cc

Additional classes – Class 1, up to 500cc, and Class 2, up to 3500cc – were recognized subsequently. Cars with compression ignition engines had a class of their own, subsequently sub-divided into the same capacity divisions as records for spark ignition vehicles; a few years ago Class K, up to 250cc, was added.

Records in these classes can be local records – the fastest times at a particular track or venue (and supplemented by the lap record and, perhaps, records over a number of laps and circuits) – or national records – the fastest speeds achieved in a particular country. But generally the aim is to establish or break international Class records, and in this book, where I have referred merely to Class records, you can take it that this was due to writer's cramp, and that an international Class record is always implied. The fastest speeds for the recognized distances or durations rank as world records. All records above national status have to be confirmed by the ruling body in Paris. America recognizes stock car records, but these are national, not international, categories.

The sub-divisions of time and distance have changed slightly down the years but are exceedingly numerous, duration records running into hundreds of days.*

*The foregoing is intended to be an explanation of motorcar records in general terms. For a full understanding of all the rules and complexities relating to them it is necessary to consult the appropriate official documents.

Why have so many men, and not a few women, spent so many hours driving round and round Brooklands and Montlhéry in pursuit of new records? The answer, nearly always, is 'bonus'. The simple fact is that manufacturers – not only of cars but also of components, accessories, fuels and oils – pay considerable sums of bonus money to those breaking records using their products. Naturally, the more important the record, the more its successful pursuit is worth, but in the formative years of the motorcar a living could be made by specializing in breaking almost any records, and it was sometimes found expedient not to go too quickly, too soon, so that a given record could be broken several times in succession by the same driver or drivers, in the same car. The importance of bonuses accounts for the mention of proprietary products other than cars in these pages: they were as much a part of record-breaking as were the vehicles.

In recent years, record-breaking has become highly specialized, because speeds in all classes have become exceedingly high and diffcult to beat, while all but the smallest cars have to be taken to temporarily closed motor roads or to the far away flats at Utah before they can be safely unleashed. So bonus money is not offered so freely as was once the case. But record-breaking attempts for publicity purposes still continue, the very long duration runs being especially favoured for this reason. In recent years Simca has gained a reputation through such activities that before the war was the proud preserve of firms such as Citroën. In the vintage years Parry Thomas earned a comfortable income mainly from royalties paid to him for successful record-breaking attempts; something few were able to do in later years, although I think George Eyston will agree that he managed it longer than anyone else! The highest form of motor racing is that which is contested over real road circuits by drivers of the highest calibre at the wheels of cars built to the prevailing Grand Prix formula, and possessing not only speed but highly developed qualities of acceleration, braking and road-holding. That I concede. But cars built for racing and record-breaking over banked tracks are also extremely fascinating. No less an authority than S C H 'Sammy' Davis has said that record-breaking is an entirely different thing from racing either on road or track, because the machine has to go faster than any other of its type or engine size has gone before, and because so often, therefore, the engine is experimental and no-one knows quite what will happen to it. The strain on both driver and car is considerable; driving literally for hours very fast round a track involves loneliness, monotony, danger from the possibility of tyre trouble or break-up of the car, and great physical strain, increased after dark, when rain, fog, snow and even ice can add to the difficulties. The car is highly stressed because the throttle is fully open, or very nearly so, the entire time, so that there is no respite for cooling and lubrication systems as in road racing.

The distances run are often altogether greater, the tyres are asked to stand up to higher speeds than have been attempted previously, and although the suspension does not have to contribute to cornering ability, the springs and chassis have to survive the pounding which defects in the bankings impose (common at Brooklands as well as at Montlhéry).

So special cars were evolved for track work, incorporating ingenious means for cutting down wind drag, cooling the oil and enclosing the driver. Such cars have maintained astonishing speeds over phenomenal distances, aided by the organized, split-second depôt work which originated when S F Edge set out to break the world's twenty-four hour record on a 60hp Napier at Brooklands in 1907, and which was perfected by Argyll, Voisin, Renault, and countless others in the competitive years that followed.

But, apart from these 'outer-circuit' cars that I find so satisfying, Montlhéry has been the scene of endurance races for sports and touring cars and innumerable club-type events, and has even been the venue, on seven occasions, for that classic contest, the French Grand Prix, which means that drivers such as Antonio Ascari, Louis Chiron, Albert Divo, Achille Varzi, Robert Benoist, Tazio Nuvolari, Jean-Pierre Wimille, Raymond Sommer, Rudolf Caracciola, and many other 'greats' have driven there.

13

Today, the track close to Paris survives and is, indeed, in almost continuous use for research purposes by the French motor industry and the military. In recent years the British — with typical seriousness of purpose — have played there in fast vintage cars, and latterly a veritable museum of French automobilism has been gathered together beneath the high bankings.

This book will, I hope, be accepted as a small tribute to this unique track; a track which has its place in motoring history and yet, happily, is still in active existence.

William Boddy
Fleet, Hampshire
January 1961

Acknowledgements

I wish to acknowledge the encouragement Lord Montagu gave me when I suggested that the series of articles on the vintage years at Montlhéry, which I wrote for his *Veteran & Vintage Magazine*, should be expanded into a book, and the helpful manner in which the archives of what is now the reference library of the Montagu Motor Museum were placed at my disposal. Lord Montagu also procured from *The Autocar* the majority of illustrations which appear in this book. I am deeply grateful to that journal for giving permission to use these copyright photographs, and for the data which I obtained from its pages. As I have said before, what would historians do without this pioneer motor journal?

I also wish to thank: Denis Jenkinson for annotating the map of Montlhéry and providing the photographs of the track's commemoration plaques; Anthony Harding of B T Batsford Ltd for lending me the rare picture of Parry Thomas in a GP Sunbeam; BMC, Jaguar, Renault, and Citroën for photographs of their cars; Fred Cann for telling me about Mrs Gwenda Hawkes and her Derby Special, and Captain George Eyston for finding time in a busy career to write the Preface.

Without such generous assistance this book would not have been possible.

The map was drawn from the UTAC plan of the course.

WB

15

AUTODROME DE

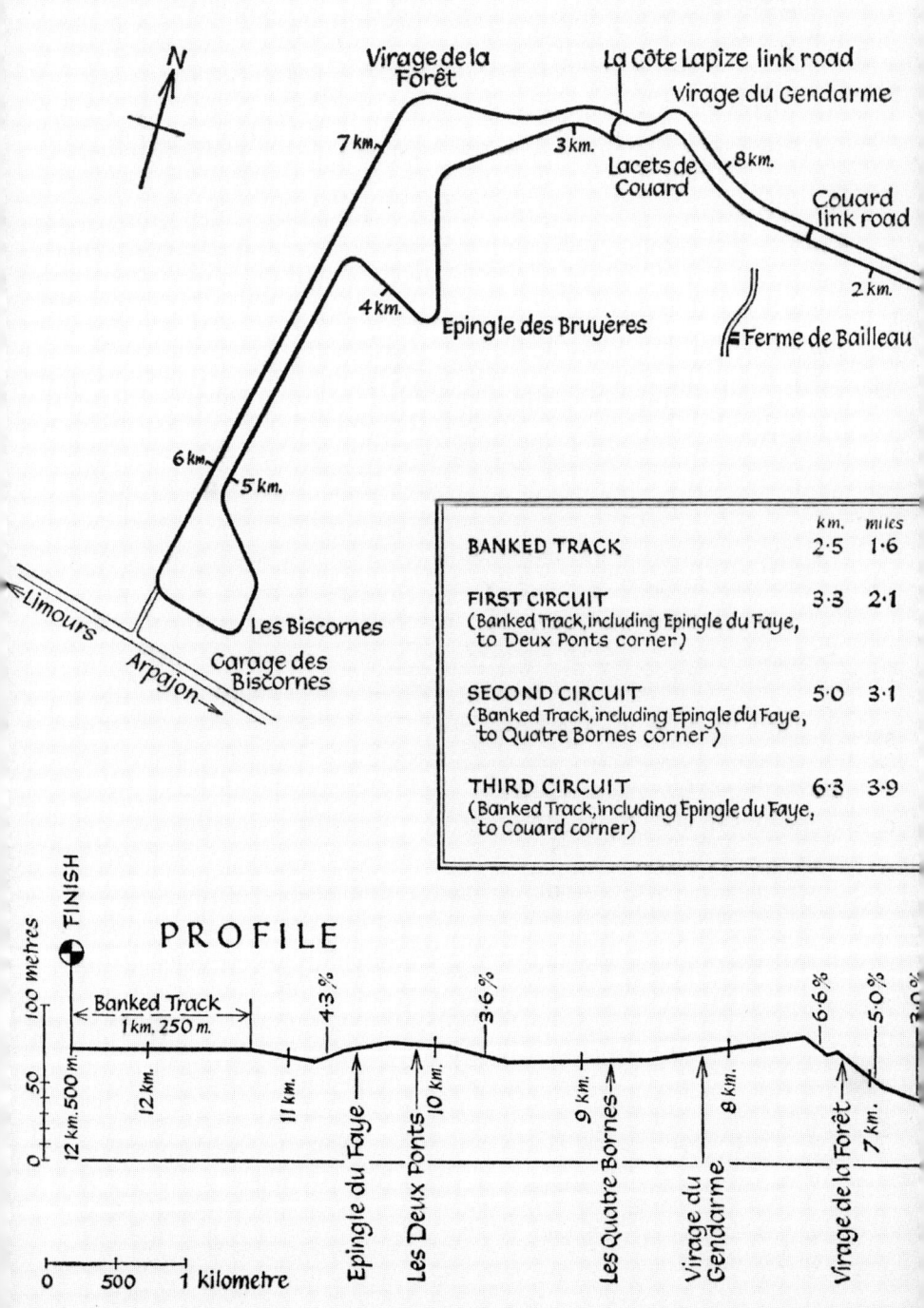

N

Virage de la Forêt

La Côte Lapize link road

Virage du Gendarme

7 km.

3 km.

Lacets de Couard

8 km.

Couard link road

4 km.

Epingle des Bruyères

2 km.

Ferme de Bailleau

6 km.

5 km.

← Limours

Arpajon →

Les Biscornes

Garage des Biscornes

	km.	miles
BANKED TRACK	2·5	1·6
FIRST CIRCUIT (Banked Track, including Epingle du Faye, to Deux Ponts corner)	3·3	2·1
SECOND CIRCUIT (Banked Track, including Epingle du Faye, to Quatre Bornes corner)	5·0	3·1
THIRD CIRCUIT (Banked Track, including Epingle du Faye, to Couard corner)	6·3	3·9

PROFILE

FINISH

100 metres

Banked Track 1 km. 250 m.

4·3%

3·6%

6·6%

5·0%

3·0%

50

12 km. 500 m.

12 km.

11 km.

Epingle du Faye

Les Deux Ponts

10 km.

9 km.

Les Quatre Bornes

Virage du Gendarme

8 km.

Virage de la Forêt

7 km.

0

0   500   1 kilometre

LINAS-MONTLHÉRY

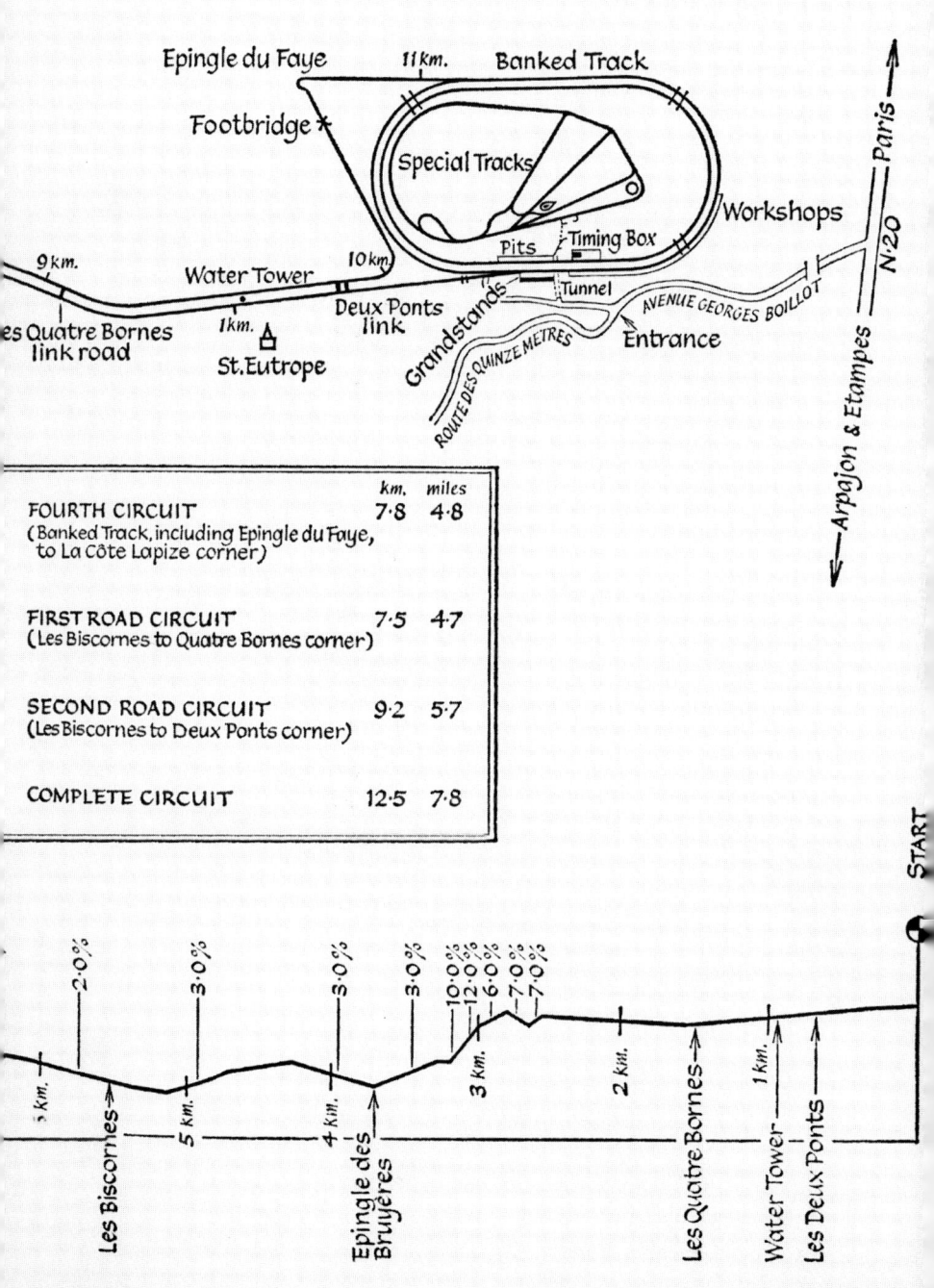

Epingle du Faye   11km.   Banked Track

Footbridge

Special Tracks

Workshops

9km.

Water Tower   10 km.

Timing Box

Pits

Deux Ponts link

es Quatre Bornes link road

1km.

St. Eutrope

Grandstands

Tunnel

ROUTE DES QUINZE METRES

AVENUE GEORGES BOILLOT

Entrance

Arpajon & Etampes

Paris

N.20

	km.	miles
FOURTH CIRCUIT (Banked Track, including Epingle du Faye, to La Côte Lapize corner)	7·8	4·8
FIRST ROAD CIRCUIT (Les Biscornes to Quatre Bornes corner)	7·5	4·7
SECOND ROAD CIRCUIT (Les Biscornes to Deux Ponts corner)	9·2	5·7
COMPLETE CIRCUIT	12·5	7·8

START

2·0%   3·0%   3·0%   3·0%   10·0% 12·0% 6·0% 7·0% 7·0%

6 km.   Les Biscornes →   5 km.   4 km.   Epingle des Bruyères   3 km.   2 km.   Les Quatre Bornes →   1 km.   Water Tower →   Les Deux Ponts →

Chapter 1

1924: the opening season

The first motor course in the world, as distinct from roads closed occasionally for racing (and if one discounts trotting and cycle tracks used for early automobile contests), was Brooklands Track in England. This 2¾-mile banked concrete track was built by the late Mr H F Locke King on his estate near Weybridge, Surrey.

It was some time before other countries built tracks but, in 1909, America followed suit with a less ambitious, only slightly banked brick circuit at Indianapolis. It was not until 1922 that Italy constructed a special motor course in Monza Park — a road circuit rather than a high-banked track — although the latter has been built at Monza in recent times. Germany built the Avus track, later with a steeply banked turn at one end, in 1922, and a very steeply banked track was constructed at Sitges in Spain in 1925.

France, where motor racing was born and where public roads could so easily be requisitioned for a motor race, did not feel the need for a closed, special course as early as some countries, but after the First World War increasing traffic density made such a track desirable; in 1924 Montlhéry Autodrome was completed.

Work was commenced, using Italian labour, on the Montlhéry track in May 1924, and it was opened for racing on 4 October, 1924. The project was financed by M Lamblin, proprietor of L' Aero Sports and owner of the Lamblin radiator manufacturing company. He bought outright a château and 12,000 acre estate on the right-hand side of the Paris-Orleans road, between the village of Linas-Montlhéry and Arpajon, on the straight tree-banked road, out of which, in 1924, the Land Speed Record was taken for the last time on the road by courageous Ernest Eldridge in the 300hp Fiat, at 146.01mph.

Thus, Montlhéry is but fifteen miles or so from Paris and consequently very conveniently situated for demonstrations and for those attending its race meetings.

M Lamblin obtained the services of a talented civil engineer, M Raymond Jamin, rather as Mr Locke King put the task of constructing Brooklands in the hands of Colonel Holden and Mr Donaldson, a railway engineer, and M Jamin set about converting the estate into a steeply-banked track of ferro-concrete, 2½ kilometres (1.58 miles) to a lap. Two bankings were joined by two brief straights, the aim being to make this the fastest track in the world. I have driven round both Brooklands and Montlhéry and, although the former was much more fun, Montlhéry being more like lapping a goldfsh bowl, there is no doubt that the French track is the faster.

Work proceeded in 1924 under the care of M Saint Macary, manager for the contractors, the Société Française de Construction, two thousand men working in two shifts from 4am to 10.30pm to lay thirty-five metres a day The château was converted into a clubhouse, lock-up garages were built actually under the arches of the home banking, so that the inmates felt and heard the thunder of racing cars passing above them, and grandstands were erected. In addition to the banked track (*La Piste de Vitesse*) a 'road' circuit (*Le Circuit Routier*) was laid down in the grounds, linked to the straights of the track via the home banking, its surface also of concrete and every sort of bend incorporated. An official aerial photograph hanging in my study confirms the lap distance of the banked track as 2584 metres.

Montlhéry was completed at a time when Brooklands Track was being hampered by complaints about noise from local residents. Silencers had been made compulsory on racing cars running at the Surrey track, motorcycle competitors had gone on strike in consequence, and anyone wishing to use Brooklands for a twenty-four-hour record or endurance attempt had to submit to the vehicle being locked away under official observation during the hours of darkness. All this undoubtedly served to focus attention

19

on Montlhéry, where speeds of up to 155mph were expected to be possible and where no restrictions existed. Moreover, the surface was considerably smoother than that of old, battle-scarred Brooklands. For all this, the promoters of the Paris track put on a rather uninspired opening meeting. They decided to have a two-day meeting over the weekend of 4-5 October, 1924, but while they probably felt that short handicap contests of the kind favoured at Brooklands would not be sufficiently auspicious, they failed to institute an important long distance race, possibly because they felt that track racing was very new and insufficient entries would be received. Instead, they settled for a series of class races of around 100 miles duration, winding up with a six-lap match race between Parry Thomas, Eldridge and Duray. The meeting opened with a race for cyclecars up to 500cc; this had but three entries and was won by Dhome's Morgan. After a 75cc lightweight motorcycle race there came a 108-mile race for 750cc small cars. This attracted an entry of four Austin Sevens from England, a Benjamin and two Sandford three wheelers, one of which was an all-enveloping 'tank' streamlined version. The Sénéchals were scratched at the last moment. The Austins, driven by E C Gordon England, Arthur Waite, Hall and Dingle, walked away with the race, finishing in that order. England averaged 73¼mph, compared to his average of 75.6mph in the 1924 200-mile race at Brooklands. The Sandford was three laps in arrears at the finish and the Benjamin and the other Sandford were flagged off with ten laps to go!

That seems to have constituted Saturday's programme.

On the Sunday racing opened with three monotonous races for motorcycles before the first car race – for light cars up to 1100cc over 124 miles – started. As the Sénéchals and Amilcars were absent the feld was composed mainly of Salmsons, but Arthur Waite sportingly ran his little green Austin Seven, although giving away 338cc. After three laps the Salmsons lapped Waite, but the Austin stayed ahead of the other French cars. Casse's Salmson led for three-quarters of the distance, then threw off its offside back tyre; during the ensuing pit stop Goutte, two years later to arouse the Brooklands crowds to enthusiasm, went ahead, to win at 85.58mph, comfortably ahead of Casse (two laps behind), while the third Salmson home, de Marnier's, was six laps behind, and Waite ten laps behind Goutte. The only real excitement was provided by a six-lap match between J G Parry Thomas's Leyland Eight, E A D Eldridge's great 300hp chain drive Fiat, and Duray's eight-cylinder 120hp D'Aoust.

It would be interesting to know more about the D'Aoust. Apparently, Automobiles J D'Aoust, of Bercham St Agathe in Belgium, was in business from about 1920 to 1925, but just what this big racing car was which Duray drove at Montlhéry remains a mystery. At all events, given a fifteen second start from Thomas, he got away badly, and was passed easily by the Leyland on the second lap, Duray cutting out and rarely using more than half the banking, which suggests either that the car was a handful, or he did not like track racing. Thomas was going splendidly, having been started fifteen seconds ahead of the Fiat, but on lap four the Leyland shed the tread from its offside back tyre. On the next lap the tyre, in ribbons, flew from the wheel. Thomas is reported as continuing at unabated speed, but whether this was bravery or a sensible desire not to run into trouble by shutting off quickly I do not know. Eldridge, the Fiat running with its new radiator and dumb-iron cowl, also lost the tread from his offside back tyre, but the cover held up, so he came in the winner, 200 yards ahead of Thomas, covering the 9.3 miles in 4 min 37.8 sec, at an average speed of 121.04mph. Thomas made the fastest lap, at 131.89mph, getting round the new track in 42.4 sec. As Montlhéry was measured three feet from the inner edge, not on a fifty foot line as at Brooklands, in fact, Thomas had lapped closer to 137mph. At the time he held the Brooklands lap record at 128.36mph.

Apart from the big-car contest, the races had come under the jurisdiction of the French motorcycle authorities,* the proposed 2-litre race having fallen through, although substantial prize

---

*Competitions for small cars and cyclecars were controlled by the French motorcycle governing body, in the same way as, in England, the ACU controlled similar activities.

money had been offered. However, later in October, a more ambitious race, over 120 laps, or 186.4 miles, was put on, confined to cars up to 1½ litres. A team of three of the 'invincible' Darracqs – entered as Talbots – ran, driven by Segrave, Scales and Bourlier, together with two La Perles, two Bugattis, two Austin Sevens, Parry Thomas's four-cylinder Thomas Special, a Buc and a Chiribin. The Talbots had it all their own way, Scales eventually taking the lead from Segrave to win at 100.3mph, with Segrave credited with fastest lap at 109.6mph. The cars crossed the line almost in formation, and, as each driver had led in turn, the result was probably prearranged. Cushman's Bugatti, fourth, was eleven laps behind the Talbots.

A big-car race over ten laps or 15½ miles was also held, which Parry Thomas won in the Leyland at 111.2mph from Vizcaya's Bugatti, 900 yards behind, with Douglas Hawkes' Ballot third, and Racowsky's Peugeot fourth. Eldridge then brought out the big Fiat

The opening meeting at Montlhéry: the start of the 1100cc race, 5 October, 1924. (The Autocar)

but was unsuccessful in breaking his own kilometre record.

However, the first of literally hundreds, if not thousands, of records fell at Montlhéry before the month was out, Gros and Martin driving a 2-litre, sixteen-valve, two-seater Bignan there for a twenty-four-hour attempt. They averaged 75.86mph for this period, covering over 1820 miles, and continued to capture the 3000km record, doing 1864 miles in all. The best lap was at 85.6mph and the greatest distance in any one hour 82¼ miles. Although the Bignan's twenty-four-hour distance was considerably less than John Duff's 'Double-Twelve' figure of over 2082 miles with the Bentley at Brooklands two years earlier, Duff had not claimed this as more than a Class record, so Gros and Martin were allowed to claim the world title, and also the sixteen-hour and all kilometre records from 1900 to 3000. An Austin Seven, in the hands of three drivers, went after the twelve-hour record but had to give up after 4hr 7min; it missed the 200-mile record but broke the Class H fifty and 100 miles and one-, three- and four-hour records.

Chapter 2

1925: the Grand Prix comes to Montlhéry

Montlhéry became active very early in 1925. It was on the afternoon of 6 January that the well-known driver Pierre Vizcaya began an attempt on Bignan's twenty-four record. Vizcaya drove a 2-litre straight-eight Bugatti. He was successful in taking class records up to 500 miles and six hours; at 82.4mph for the 500 miles. He continued into the night, which was fine, with bright moonlight. Alas, it was also very cold, and just before ten hours had elapsed a very hard frost coated the track with a sheet of ice. Soon afterwards Vizcaya's difficulties increased when a tyre burst. The Bugatti slid down the steep banking, the driver lost control, and the car rolled over several times. By a miracle Vizcaya escaped with a few bruises but Bignan retained the record.

Racing commenced at Montlhéry on 17 May with a 300-mile race for unsupercharged cars up to 1500cc, weighing at least 550kg. The idea of banning the now popular supercharger was no doubt to keep out the unbeatable Talbot-Darracqs. Entries were accepted at 10,000 francs, 7000 of which was returnable if the car started – starting money, in effect – and prize money totalled 150,000 francs. Cars had to run in their national colours; private entries to be distinguished by a white nose.

The Talbots *did* start, in unblown form, handled by Segrave, Duller and Conelli. Segrave was held back by tyre trouble, but Duller led comfortably, with the amateur Conelli behind him. This GP de l'Ouverture had a truly memorable finish. On the last lap, with the track now slippery due to rain that had fallen for the past hour mixing with clay soil blown from the unfinished infield, Conelli tried to pass Duller. His blue Talbot skidded, the offside back wheel hitting the outer retaining wall, which caused the car to spin round twice and overturn. It finally left the track and settled back on its wheels in the infield. For some reason the spectators hissed and jeered George Duller, who was entirely blameless. Conelli was able to walk to the ambulance and got away with superficial leg injuries, but an official was crushed by the Talbot as it hit the wall, and had to have a leg amputated. The car was scarcely damaged and Moriceau drove it back to Paris. Sixteen cars started. Duller drove non-stop to win at 97.2mph for the 312 miles. Segrave was third, seven miles behind, Conelli being granted second place as, before his crash, he crossed the line a length behind Duller. Eldridge's side-valve Eldridge Special, with 'Eldridge cowl' over the radiator, had been delayed by tyre trouble, but speeded up in the wet to finish fourth, twenty laps behind the winner. Thomas at first remained up with the Talbots, until his Thomas Special developed magneto trouble. R C Morgan's slower Thomas Special retired with a blown gasket. The French cars were mostly pathetic. The Salmsons retired after a mere twelve laps, and the La Perles, the Jean Gras and the six-cylinder Bucs were in continual trouble, Lefevre's La Perle (or Le Perle) overturning. Eventually, Jonay's Jean Gras finished fifth, fifty laps in arrears, and Bucciali's Buc sixth, fifty-two laps behind Duller.

It was for this race that Ettore Bugatti built two straight-eight, 1½-litre cars devoid of back springs. He drove one himself from Molsheim, but his theory that rubber blocks could replace leaf springs at Montlhéry was soon proved completely false and the cars were withdrawn. Other non-starters were A G Miller's Aston Martin and all four Chiribiris.

After this rather dull long distance race the spectators were treated to a six-lap triangular match race between Eldridge's gigantic Fiat, Parry Thomas' Leyland, and a Borgenschutz Special with a 180hp Hispano-Suiza aero engine under its bonnet. The last named petered out, the Fiat burst its offside back tyre after four laps, and Parry Thomas won happily, at 126mph. Fastest lap in the previous race had been made by Segrave, at 106.1mph.

Meanwhile, much record activity had been witnessed at Montlhéry. Incidentally, the lap distance was now measured almost on the centre line of the track, and the Bignan of 1924 was credited with averaging 77.3mph (1801.98 miles) in the twenty-four hours.

Sunbeam planned to break this record, and the 2-litre GP car with which Segrave won at San Sebastian the previous year was provided with a higher axle ratio for the purpose.

Segrave, Parry Thomas and Conelli were appointed to drive, and the plot was to average 100mph throughout, stopping every four hours to refuel, change all tyres and put in a fresh driver. The attempt started in the early morning of 22 February, with snow coating the top of the bankings. Every kind of bad weather was enveloping Paris at the time, but Segrave, accompanied by a riding mechanic, got going well, breaking class records for fifty kilometres, fifty miles, 100 kilometres and 100 miles, all at over 100mph, the last three in excess of 101mph. Segrave continued, taking world records for three hours and 500 kilometres at over 102mph: clearly, the Sunbeam was going extremely fast, but when Thomas took over snow began to fall more heavily, and even had engine trouble not stopped the attempt after 4hr 35min 26sec, undoubtedly the weather would have done.

Britain finally regained the world twenty-four-hour record when T Gillettt – who used to own a café on the Portsmouth road – took out a single-seater, 2-litre AC, with typically long tail and high-sided cockpit, immediately after the finish of racing on 17 May. The thunderstorms which had contributed to Conelli's accident persisted, and the night was very dark: Gillett's task not being rendered any easier by inadequate lighting of the track. The AC ran magnificently, lapping with astonishing regularity. Gillett drove the whole distance himself, being massaged during the brief depôt stops and eating grapes and biscuits. He lopped off record after record from Bignan, whose engineers and drivers were present the whole time and warm in their praise of Gillett's stamina. The AC stopped every three hours for fuel and oil, and needed on one occasion considerable water. The Dunlop tyres stood up splendidly, with no failures experienced and only six fresh tyres fitted. The car was stationary for only 1hr 4min, and the only trouble was with a faulty plug. Gillett went on after the twenty-four-hours to capture the 2000 mile record. The twenty-four-hour record was taken at 81.27mph (1949.3 miles) and 81.3mph was averaged for the 2000 miles.

Gillett found Montlhéry smoother than Brooklands, but more tiring to drive because of the absence of long straights. His attempt was supervised by S F Edge, Sydney Smith, the Hon Victor Bruce, and Norman Freeman of Dunlop. Incidentally, Montlhéry was not closed for the attempt, a Rolland-Pilain, Panhard-Levassor, the Thomas Special and Gwenda Stewart's Rudge-Whitworth motorcycle going round while the AC was making its run.

Fearful after Conelli's crash, the officials fussed about Gillett continuing for the 2000-mile record, threatening to close the track if more rain fell – and this fine attempt ended in another thunderstorm and drenching rain.

Before this the Renault company, which had given up competition participation many years before, decided that as Montlhéry was so near Paris it had better make an effort. One of Renault's fabulous 9-litre, 45hp chassis was fitted with an open four-seater body. Driven by Garfield and Plessier, it broke seventeen records, some of them world records, including covering 500 miles at nearly 104mph. Later, the car was credited with the Class A twelve- and twenty-four-hour records, at 97.94mph and 87.63mph respectively.

Another match race was staged in June 1925 between the same three cars as in May, together with Albert Divo at the wheel of the big vee-twelve Delage, later driven in this country by Cobb, Bertram, Kay Petre and Cecil Clutton. The Delage averaged 125½mph for the 9.3 miles, beating the Leyland and Fiat in that order. Moreover, Divo put in a new lap record at 136.3mph (4.1.8sec), beating the previous best, which Parry Thomas had set up, of 135.07mph.

Thomas later broke four short distance records with the Leyland-Thomas, from five kilometres to ten miles. The French Grand Prix was to be held over the Montlhéry track-and-road circuit. The latter was ready well in advance of the race, the thirty-three feet wide roads being macadam treated with coldspray on foundations formed of sand, hard stone quarried in the neighbourhood and granite, some of which came from as far away as Brittany. 2500 workers, with a further 700 engaged on the entrance roads, pushed forward the work, which continued until 2am each day under floodlights. Forty-five five-ton lorries, eighteen miles of railway and twelve tractors were involved; Montlhéry track and road circuit are said to have cost £500,000 together.

The 1925 French Grand Prix was run over 621 miles, utilizing one of the track's bankings. Originally the road circuit was to have been lapped left-handed but this was altered and the turns were taken right-handed. The Grand Prix was expected to be an extremely strenuous race. It was supported by a motorcycle Grand Prix and a Touring Car Grand Prix under fuel consumption rules the previous weekend, and special arrangements were made to get traffic to and from Paris by three main one-way routes.

The Touring Car Grand Prix, held on 19 July, had generated considerable interest amongst several of the leading French manufacturers, perhaps because it was Montlhéry's first major road race. The rules stipulated that the competing cars should carry ballast equivalent to full passenger capacity, but there were no restrictions on specification. The 5-litre cars had to carry the equivalent of six passengers, cover a distance of 652 miles, and had a petrol allowance equal to 12.8mpg. The 3-litre cars were ballasted to equal four passengers, had to run 621 miles, and achieve a minimum of 15.7mpg. The 1½-litre class was required to travel 590 miles at a fuel consumption of at least 24mpg but need only carry the equivalent of two passengers.

The 5-litre class drew entries of three Peugeots and three Steyrs, the 3-litre class was confined to a trio of Cottin-Desgouttes, as the Diatto entries were withdrawn at the last moment, and the 1½-litre class saw five Bugattis, three Darracqs, three Mathis and two EHPS face the starter. Only one driver per car was permitted and he could not receive outside assistance.

Mathis had built special cars for the race, and had made a big effort to reduce wind-drag to a minimum, consistent with certain minimum body regulations which had to be observed and the weight limit in the 1½-litre class of 12cwt 89lb empty.

A special chassis frame was used, drastically unswept from the centre forward, to keep the centre of gravity very low, the driver sitting on the offside well below the line of the propeller-shaft tunnel. The car was crab-tracked and had a very narrow radiator, but a very wide body at the centre enclosing the back wheels, and with a long tail. Detachable panels enabled the back wheels to be changed if necessary, air directed round the tyres was let out via louvres in the end of the tail, and further louvres in bonnet and scuttle got rid of hot air drawn in through the radiator. The front wheels were covered by cycle-type wings turning with them: the general appearance of these Touring Grand Prix Mathis cars was rather untidy.

The chassis was that of the well-known four-cylinder, 69 x 100mm model with vertical overhead valves actuated by a chain-driven overhead camshaft, the engine having two Solex carburetters, pump cooling, pump and splash lubrication, and two plugs per cylinder served by Delco coil ignition. The drive passed through a multi-plate clutch to a unit four-speed and reverse gearbox, an open shaft taking the drive to the back axle. Perrot-type front wheel brakes, half-elliptic suspension damped by Hartford shock-absorbers, and Rudge-Whitworth detachable wire wheels shod with 765 x 105 Michelin tyres completed the specification. Two spare wheels were accommodated in the tail, vertically one each side of the differential housing, within the capacious streamlined tail. The underparts of the car were enclosed by a flat fairing and, as part of the race had to be contested at night, headlamps were carried.

Peugeot also prepared special cars for the Touring Car Grand Prix, based on its standard 18hp sleeve-valve chassis with raised compression ratio, enlarged ports, a special carburetter, and modified lubrication system. These lhd chassis were endowed with imposing streamlined saloon bodies built under Weymann licence by the Lagache and Glazmann Company in Paris, and covered in blue leather cloth. Peugeot considered that better streamlining could be achieved in this way than by using the conventional open touring bodywork.

The windscreen was a very pronounced vee, each panel a single pane hinged at the top, and the windscreen pillars had a rearward inclination. The upper part of this saloon had a streamlined rear end devoid of a back window that blended with a streamlined tail in which two spare wheels were accommodated horizontally. The undershield extended in one piece from the front dumb-irons to the extremity of the tail.

There were two doors; one at the back nearside giving access to the rear compartment of the body, and the other on the front offside for access to the driving seat. Big helmet-type front mudguards swivelled with the centre-lock wire wheels; at the back normal wings – blending with wide running-boards – were used.

The back of the body was taken up with two vast petrol reservoirs, one twice as tall as the other, giving a total capacity of forty gallons, as refuelling was not allowed during the race: would that this rule had led to a better fuel range from today's production cars! The headlamps of these Peugeots were concealed within the scuttle sides and could be swung out when required, otherwise concealed by fairings.

It is amusing to find that although this was called the Touring Car Grand Prix, the rules ignored the chassis specification, so that one Darracq was a racing car rigged up with touring equipment and a dynamo in place of its Roots supercharger, while the Bugatti entries included road-equipped straight-eight Grand Prix models.

Around 8.30am on the day of the race the competing cars,

their petrol tanks full and sand-bagged with the requisite ballast, were towed out on to the track by Citroën-Kégresse tractors.

Engines had to be started via electric starter which did not please some of the Bugatti drivers. Poor Colas discovered that a front tyre of his Cottin-Desgouttes was flat and had to set about inflating it with a hand pump while the others roared away. D'Aulun's EHP was first away, followed by Bocchi's Mathis and the disguised racing Darracq driven by Bourlier.

The Darracq was first back after a lap had been completed, chased by Kinsky's white Weymann fabric-bodied open Steyr and Bocchi's Mathis.

The big cars, headed by two Steyrs, soon passed the smaller machines and the race was not particularly exciting to watch, fastest lap (by Boillot's Peugeot) as slow as 57.2mph, with fuel conservation in mind.

After an hour Wagner's Peugeot had fallen out with engine trouble and the Russian driver Ivanowsky had brought his Mathis in with leaking water pipes. He resourcefully tore up his gloves, bound the porous piping with them, and then replenished with all the liquids carried in the car: drinking water, cola and coffee! But this isn't how motor races are won; the leaks persisted and the car had to retire. The other Mathis also suffered from loss of water and petrol and de Bronnond and Bocchi both retired.

Bourlier's racing Darracq had to be left at the roadside with defective steering, Lacharnay's Cottin-Desgouttes, while running second to the Steyr, burst a tyre, causing the team manager to slow his other cars. Then the Steyrs were in real trouble with the tubes in their enormous Michelin 'Comfort' tyres, which seems to have been anticipated as each driver was provided with two spare wheels: two spare covers in the tail, spare tubes and a compressed air bottle. Even so, each puncture lost the driver twenty minutes.

André Boillot thus took the lead for Peugeot, was challenged by Vizcaya's straight-eight Bugatti until the GP car suffered from radiator leaks, and by half distance the Peugeot saloons of Boillot and Rigal led from the best of the Cottin-Desgouttes.

The race may have been instructive from the manufacturers' points of view, but it was horribly dull for those watching it.

Although the weather was ideal, *The Autocar*'s reporter counted only about a score of spectators in the big grandstands at the start, and by noon the actual number was fifty-nine, inclusive of soldiers and attendants. As the race did not end until after dark it can be imagined how few people stayed to see the winners home! In fact, the organizers had asked for a special train from Paris and 1400 buses; the train brought twenty-one spectators, and only fifty buses were needed. After the race one Montlhéry hotel was left with 400 plucked chickens on its hands!

Benoist (EHP) and Bourlier, now in Chassagne's Darracq, ran out of petrol and weren't allowed to take on supplies. Ledu's Darracq suffered the same fate, but, being only three-quarters of a mile from the finish, the luckless driver pushed it over the line.

André Boillot was the hero of the race, driving his Peugeot alone and going on for an extra lap after being signalled to finish, so that he was at the wheel for 12½ hours. A little drama relieved the latter part of the race. The open cars were required to run one lap with hoods erect, but two of the improvised Darracqs were already in trouble with broken windscreen supports which made it necessary to reduce speed. They lost considerable time, and worried everyone in the pit, when their hoods had to be held up with rope. Delalande's Cottin-Desgouttes lost much oil, but the driver emptied the gallon of water he had aboard into the sump and got the car home. The results were declared as:

5000cc Class (652 miles)
1st   A Boillot (Peugeot) 12hr 12min 39⅕sec, 53.3mph
2nd   Gauderman (Steyr) 12hr 55min 48⅕sec
3rd   L Rigal (Peugeot) 12hr 59min 23⅘sec

3000cc Class (621.3 miles)
1st   Lacharnay (Cottin-Desgouttes) 11hr 40min 40⅖sec, 53.1mph

2nd   Colas (Cottin-Desgouttes) 12hr 22min 14⅕sec
3rd   Delalande (Cottin-Desgouttes) 12hr 32min 13⅗sec

1500cc Class (590.3 miles)

1st   Constantini (Bugatti) 11hr 12min 7⅖sec
2nd   de Vizcaya (Bugatti) 11hr 21min 11⅕sec
3rd   Foresti (Bugatti) 11hr 43min 48⅕sec
4th   Goux (Bugatti)
5th   Ledu (Darracq)

Constantini drove a roller-bearing straight-eight GP Bugatti which finished with a very clean engine. The other Bugattis were also of this type and all went through without changing the Michelin tyres.

The French Grand Prix, held a week later, was rather more of a success, although because it had not been advertised extensively, and those Parisians who can do so tend to leave the capital about the middle of June, it is doubtful whether more than 25,000 spectators saw this exciting race.

This was the last great race to be run in France under the 2-litre formula, and it attracted a good entry, which formed up on the starting grid as follows:

P de Vizcaya	Campari	Segrave
(Bugatti)	*(Alfa-Romeo)*	*(Sunbeam)*
Ascari	Count Masetti	Divo
(Alfa-Romeo)	*(Sunbeam)*	*(Delage)*
Count Conelli	Benoist	Goux
(Sunbeam)	*(Delage)*	*(Bugatti)*
Wagner	Constantini	Brilli-Peri
(Delage)	*(Bugatti)*	*(Alfa-Romeo)*

Foresti   F de Vizcaya
(Bugatti)   *(Bugatti)*

The Delage cars were the fabulous twin Roots-supercharged, roller-bearing, vee-twelve 51.1 x 80mm cars, developing over 150bhp, although their drivers were restricting maximum engine speed to 5800-6300rpm during the race.

The Sunbeams were the six-cylinder Roots-supercharged cars developed from the non-supercharged 2-litres of which Segrave's had won the French Grand Prix for Britain for the first time at Tours in 1I923. The Alfa-Romeos were the highly successful supercharged straight-eight P2 cars, and only the straight-eight Bugattis were without blowers.

There were three non-starters: a Thomas Special; a Mathis, and one of the Delage cars. The five Bugattis were nearly scratched because the organizers said their cowled-over mechanic's seats didn't comply with the regulations, and it was not until the last minute that Ettore Bugatti agreed to this cowling being cut back and tucked in. Of the fourteen drivers contesting this 620-mile race over Montlhéry's road-cum-track circuit, eight were Italian (Divo was claimed to be of this nationality on this occasion).

A Peugeot saloon and a Mathis saloon led the snarling pack on a rather ragged rolling start, from which Antonio Ascari's red Alfa-Romeo emerged in the lead by several hundred yards from Divo's Delage, Masetti's Sunbeam in third.

Ascari began to pull out a substantial lead, his Alfa-Romeo devouring the high banking at 120mph. Behind, his team-mates moved up; Campari to third place, Brilli-Peri to sixth position.

Divo's Delage was the first to pay a call at the sunk pits for a plug change and attention to the carburetter, which lost him a lap. After five laps Ascari led very comfortably from Campari. Wagner's Delage was third, and Masetti's Sunbeam fourth.

The Sunbeams and Delages were well matched but clearly the P2 Alfa-Romeos were the fastest cars on the course, although Brilli-Peri's needed an early plug change, minor adjustments and water. At the same time Divo was in again for the Delage's carburetter jets to be changed.

By ten laps Ascari had lapped Conelli's Sunbeam, and the next time round set a lap record of 5min 49sec, or just over 80mph. Divo went out with supercharger trouble, and, as a drizzling rain began to fall, P de Vizcaya called for goggles.

Ascari is said to have signalled to his pit by cutting his engine in and out when passing the pits, and next time round he stopped for both back wheels to be changed in 2min 8sec.

When the Alfa-Romeo continued it was still in the lead, but Campari now closer to it, with Wagner and Benoist behind in the Delage cars. Campari then made a pit-stop to have the back wheels changed and take on petrol and a little water. The Alfa-Romeo was stationary for 2min 29sec, the officials stopping it as it was moving off to make the pit mechanic clear away from the track all the tools he had been using.

Count Conelli's Sunbeam was the next retirement, with a defect in the servo brakes.

Now, alas, tragedy intervened. After leading the Grand Prix brilliantly for 169 miles, Ascari had somehow lost control of his car whilst taking the long left bend at the end of the straight. The Alfa-Romeo had hit the paling fence, torn it down for 130 yards and, with the wheels now on soft earth, overturned into the ditch. Ascari was put in a military ambulance but died on the way to Paris.

The race went on, Campari now leading Divo in Benoist's Delage and Masetti's Sunbeam. These cars were separated by about four minutes between each, and, although Divo was driving hard, it was claimed that this Delage had needed a new crankshaft and bearings before the race, which were not run-in.

Campari and Brilli-Peri were both at their pits when the sad news reached Montlhéry that Ascari was dead. As a token of respect the engines of both Alfa-Romeos were revved, then silenced for the rest of the day.

In drizzling rain, which made for uncomfortable viewing for the spectators in the unroofed grandstands, Divo did his utmost for Delage, setting a new lap record of 5min 48sec (80.3mph) in spite of the slippery conditions.

The battle now lay between the two Delage cars, with relief drivers for each, and Masetti, who elected to go the whole distance himself in the green Sunbeam. Unfortunately, the floorboards of Masetti's car became detached towards the end, preventing the throttle from opening fully, and resulting in a brief pit-stop. The two blue cars were now firmly in the lead and the President of the Republic saw Benoist take a very popular victory, France's first French Grand Prix victory since 1913.

The results were:

1st	Robert Benoist/Albert Divo (Delage) 8hr 54min, 4½sec, 69.7mph
2nd	Louis Wagner (Delage) 9hr 2min 27⅖sec, 68.7mph
3rd	Count Masetti (Sunbeam) 9hr 6min. 15⅕sec, 68.2mph
4th	M Constantini (Bugatti) 9hr 7 min 38sec 68⅖mph
5th	J Goux (Bugatti) 9hr 15min 11⅕sec
6th	F de Vizcaya (Bugatti) 9hr 20min 48⅖sec
7th	P de Vizcaya (Bugatti) 9hr 41min 1⅗sec
8th	J Foresti (Bugatti) 9hr 49min 38⅗ sec

Retired: Divo (Delage), supercharger; Ascari (Alfa-Romeo) fatal accident; Conelli (Sunbeam) brake trouble; Segrave (Sunbeam) broken inlet valve.

Meanwhile, there had been activity over on the outer circuit. A Panhard of 20hp sports type set out on an attempt on the world hour record, but, although it lapped at 118mph, a tyre burst after some sixty miles put paid to the attempt. However, before retiring the Panhard broke Class records for fifty kilometres, fifty miles, and 100 kilometres. Later, the Panhard-Levassor company was successful with Ortmans claiming the Class C hour record at 110.31mph. Robert Benoist had the big 10½-litre vee-twelve Delage out and broke the flying start five mile, five kilometre and ten kilometre records held previously by Parry Thomas' Leyland-Thomas. The five miles were covered at 133mph.

Apart from such sprint records and the hard task of trying to break the hour record, several people had their eyes on the twenty-four-hour record held by the Renault 45 at 87.63mph. John Duff prepared a 3-litre Bentley in which to attempt it, asking Dr J D Benjafield to share the long drive with him.The car had a special engine and lightweight Weymann single-seater fabric body, with high-sided cockpit and tail.

The Bentley started near to darkness, and drizzly rain — which turned to a heavy downpour — did not ease the drivers' task. The 1000-mile record was taken from Renault at 97.7mph but the twelve-hour record was missed by a mere twelve kilometres. No 3 exhaust pipe caused delay by breaking away; one stop being necessary to jury-rig it and another to make a more permanent repair. Alas, after it had been running for 18¼ hours the Bentley had to give up, the bottom bevel of the timing gear having failed. AC also made an attempt on the twenty-four-hour record, and no doubt smarted under the defeat, by 6.36mph, of Gillett's record by a car of six litres greater capacity. However, the AC gave up comparatively early, although no-one was informed as to the cause.

As Motor Show time approached record activity at Montlhéry really began to warm up, for the resultant publicity was deemed beneficial to sales, and the pilgrimage provided an excuse to visit Paris before facing the rigours of Olympia and the English winter. Duff repaired his Bentley, took Woolf Barnato as his partner this time, and, late in September of 1925, won from Renault the world twenty-four-hour record, at the truly creditable speed of 95.02mph, the British car covering 2280.9 miles without the bonnet being opened. For lap after lap the Bentley circulated at 96.6mph, hardly varying from this speed, which represented fifty-nine seconds exactly on the stopwatches. Every three hours the car came in for replenishment and a change of driver. Montlhéry lived up to its reputation, low fog hampering Duff and Barnato during the night, seriously reducing visibility. The Dunlop straight-sided tyres were changed only when necessary: two rears, which had covered some 500 miles in practice after nine hours, and those on the front wheels after twenty-one hours. A whistle from the time-keeper's box told when the Renault's speed had been equalled and thereafter Duff improved on the old record.

The last depôt stop took only seventy-one seconds and the bonnet remained closed throughout the attempt. This was a particularly creditable effort, as the Bentley was not works sponsored.

While this splendidly conducted and successful twenty-four-hour run was in progress Colonel and Mrs Stewart set off round Montlhéry on their own twenty-four-hour record bid, with a Rudge-Whitworth motorcycle. However, a strong wind deterred them and the piston broke after some five hours. Garfield put in some laps in a Renault and the Voisin staff were active, preparing for a twenty-four-hour record attempt on the following day.

This Voisin, a sleeve-valve 18hp car, set out eighteen hours after the Bentley had stopped, the drivers — Lefèvre, Marchand and Julienne — swopping every three hours. A very fast pace was set with the first hour's average of 100.37mph compared to Duff's 94.6mph and the big Renault's 91.9mph. The world six-hour record fell at 100.4mph, the 1000 kilometre record was broken at 100.3mph and, after 1500 kilometres, the Voisin had bettered the Bentley's speed but did not beat the Renault's record, the latter car not having slowed until twenty-one hours. It looked as if the British car's newly-won fame would be shortlived, but from 2000 kilometres on the French car slowed and, after 16hr 5min (1525.8 miles) it stopped altogether with mechanical maladies. The Voisin, however, had secured four Class C records as well as two world honours.

Next it was the turn of Panhard-Levassor, and this time Ortmans was successful. His tuned sports model shattered five world and five Class C records in the course of an hour's run, in which the world hour record rose to the astonishing figure of 115.3mph. This beat Parry Thomas' speed for the hour by 4.7mph.

In October 1925, Montlhéry was the scene of small-car races over the road circuit, Doré's Sénéchal defeating the Salmsons in the 1100cc category and Violet, driving one of his curious flat-twin two-strokes, winning the 750cc class. The 500cc category was exciting because Doré and Stanton contrived to dead-heat, each driving a Sima-Violet, their mechanics holding hands as the cars crossed the line (Formula 3 drivers were to revive this custom many years later!). The Sénéchal averaged 61.7mph, Violet 56.2mph, defeating Hall's Austin Seven which had to start without its water pump, and the half-litre Sima-Violets managed 48.5mph. At this meeting Divo, with a 6-litre Delage and Benoist in the vee- twelve GP Delage, gave demonstrations on the outer circuit to raise funds for a dead driver's widow, and, as night came on, a Rolland-Pilain commenced a run intended to continue for six days and six nights without respite! The car concerned was a 2-litre with lightweight saloon body. It had to give up after forty-nine hours, but, during that time, took the world 2500-mile record at 63.59mph and collected Class records for 4000 and 5000 kilometres. Twenty-four hours later this Rolland-Pilain was off again, claiming Class records up to one hour.

Rather faster, Ernest Eldridge brought his supercharged side-valve Eldridge Special to Montlhéry and broke similar records in the 1½-litre class, covering 172 kilometres (199.62 miles) in the hour. Later, further records in this class fell to Eldridge, including the five and ten miles, the latter at 116.5mph. This beat records held by Segrave (Darracq), and Eldridge's sv car lapped at no less than 116.97mph.

Louis Renault had given orders that his firm must regain the world twenty-four-hour record. The first attempt failed because of a water leak around the cylinder head, but not before Garfield, the American, and Plessier, the French driver, had been lapping for twelve hours at 100.45mph, taking records for 1000, 1500 and 2000 kilometres and 1000 miles.

While preparing for an attempt on the hour record, the indefatigable Eldridge had another go at shorter distances, improving on his own records from five kilometres to ten miles, achieving over 120mph for all save the last-named distance, which he covered at 119.87mph. The sv Anzani-engined car now lapped at 120.67mph,

The situation at Renault Frères must have become tense in November, because, choosing an isolated fine day, Marchand and

Lefevre took out an 18hp sleeve-valve Voisin and broke all of the 45hp Renault's records up to six hours (635.21 miles). Then, working his way up, Eldridge took from Parry Thomas the world fifty-kilometre record, at 116.4:3mph. In December the Eldridge Special went faster still, with a lap timed at 124.7mph while raising the five-kilometre to ten-mile records. He left the five- and ten-mile records at 121½mph.

Eldridge next played a very cunning hand. In 1926 a new ruling was to be enforced, preventing a car in one international engine capacity class from breaking records in any other classes. Before this came into force, Eldridge took out the Eldridge Special to attempt Class E (1500-2000cc) records) having ballasted it with 2cwt to bring it above the minimum 650kg weight stipulated for that class. He broke two records, established two fresh ones, and, after the engine had been officially measured, and found to be under 1500cc, was credited with the Class F records also!

A fortnight later the ingenious Ernest Eldridge was out again, his little car — which had a Gordon England fabric streamlined body — now weighing in at 550kg, the minimum for Class F. Eldridge established four new records in that category, for five and ten kilometres and five and ten miles, but was slower than before, probably because a stiff wind was blowing that Christmas Eve of 1925, when the attempt was made.

After this Eldridge decided that the car had reached its peak in side valve form.

Montlhéry was established as a record-breaking centre.

*Reducing wind resistance: the 1½-litre Mathis for the Touring Car Grand Prix of 1925. (*The Autocar*)*

*Touring Car Grand Prix of 1925: André Boillot's winning Peugeot. (*The Autocar*)*

*A Cottin-Desgouttes is followed by a Peugeot saloon during the 1925 event. (*The Autocar*)*

Parry Thomas in the 2-litre GP Sunbeam, 1925.
(Monde et Caméra/BT Bauford Ltd)

Chapter 3

1926: twenty-four hours at a hundred

The 1926 season at Montlhéry opened with a successful record attempt by Lefevre in a 4-litre sleeve-valve Voisin, which beat Eldridge's fifty-kilometre record of 116.9mph, and Parry Thomas' fifty mile Brooklands record of 118.059mph.

Renault was still intent on recapturing the world twenty-four-hour record and had built a very impressive Renault 45 for the purpose. This was a single-seater streamlined saloon, in contrast to the open four-seater that took this coveted record at 87.63mph, until beaten by Duff's 3-litre Bentley, which averaged 95.02mph.

This Renault 45 saloon was, in my opinion, one of the most exciting-looking track cars ever built. It was based on the standard 110 x 160mm (9123cc) Renault 45 chassis, which, in any case, was a pretty intriguing motor car, its big, side-by-side valve power unit with alloy pistons, duralumin connecting rods and a lubrication system incorporating an oil radiator and centrifugal oil cleaner, not to mention a duralumin back axle with steel liners. One of these great chassis was prepared, with 2:1 axle ratio and mild engine tuning, and was fitted with a low, slim, single-seater closed body, the roof of which merged into the pointed tail. This body was made of fabric-leather and weighed only 134lb with a height of 5ft 7in.

The gear and brake levers were set to the left of the driver's seat, and in the tail were a fifty-five gallon petrol tank and an auxiliary oil tank. Nearly eight gallons of oil were carried.

Thermo-syphon cooling was retained but the scuttle radiator was sharply raked. This raises a nice point for motoring historians. In Saint Loup's book on Renault it is recounted how Plessier, head of the testing department, admitted in fear and trepidation to

Louis Renault that, on the record-breaking 45hp car, he had to put the radiator in front, to achieve efficient cooling. Saint Loup goes on to tell his readers that, instead of sacking Plessier, Renault rushed to the drawing office and demanded that all the models be forthwith provided with radiators in the conventional location! Contemporary reports confirm that the radiator remained in the scuttle of the Montlhéry saloon, and illustrations suggest that the front of the long bonnet was closed by wire mesh. The only possible explanation is that a front radiator was found necessary at the last moment but that the press was not encouraged to notice it ...

Reverting to the record car, the engine used three carburetters, each feeding via a Y-shaped manifold. It is interesting, in view of modern developments of placing carburetter intakes in cold-air boxes, that horizontal and vertical plates on the inside of the nearside of the Renault's bonnet formed separate compartments; one for the carburetters, and the one above for the manifolds and exhaust stubs. Exhaust heat was applied to the manifolds but boiling of fuel in the float chambers was obviated.

At the front of the chassis Renault hydraulic shock absorbers were fitted, while the underslung cantilever back springs were damped by triple Hartfords mounted on spherical attachments. To avoid steering shimmy the front brakes were removed but the gearbox-driven servo was retained for the back brakes.

The drivers were able to observe the front tyres through the windows in the doors, and mirrors were so fixed that they could also see the condition of the back tyres. The facia contained a maximum throttle setting to prevent accidental over-revving, and instruments were confined to inlet and outlet water thermometers and an oil thermometer. If it was considered that the sump required replenishment, the driver could operate a tap behind him which lowered a fresh supply of oil by gravity to the engine.

This Renault weighed no less than 2tons 4cwt 70lb ready for action, and it was found that the 33 x 5 straight-sided tyres would have to be changed every hour, whereas it had been originally hoped that the car could continue for two-hour spells.

Fourteen carefully trained men stood by. At each depôt stop two worked on each wheel, three filled the petrol tank through a filler in the roof, another filled the radiator, and yet another checked the oil, while the fourteenth man kept a general watch to see that all was well. The car was lifted on four jacks, operated simultaneously. Refuelling was from a pneumatic-tyred tank at which one man maintained air pressure, one held the supply hose, and the third directed the nozzle into the car's tank. The shortest depôt stop during the twenty-four-hour record attempt occupied only fifty-two seconds, but it was estimated that each stop cost three minutes, allowing for slowing down and regaining speed.

Tyre life was the primary worry, because a burst tyre would mean doing a lap on the rim, with the possibility of wheel failure. Consequently a limit of 2250rpm was imposed during the hours of darkness, and 2300rpm during daylight. In fact, the Renault had a maximum speed in the region of 120mph. The electric starter was used to restart the engine after each depôt stop.

Garfield, the American driver, put in a preliminary appearance with the big Renault and broke the world 100 kilometre record at 117.36mph, previously held by Parry Thomas. Before Garfield was ready to tackle the twenty-four-hour record, Ortmans took out a straight-eight sleeve valve 85 x 140mm (6355cc) Panhard-Levassor at Montlhéry and broke the world fifty kilometre, fifty mile and 100 kilometre records: all three were taken from Voisin and Renault at over 124mph. The Panhard was of sports type, with enlarged ports, modified timing, higher compression ratio and 165mm Michelin semi-balloon tyres. For the first time a speed of 200kph had been maintained in a series of records taken at Montlhéry.

A few days later Ortmans raised his own 100 kilometre record to 125.38mph. This was merely a warm-up for an attempt on the world hour record, which the Panhard duly achieved, first at 115.44mph, then at 120.244mph, the first time over 120 miles had been covered in the hour. Ortmans, an amateur driver, also increased the 100-mile record to 123.69mph; he drove the 6¼-litre 40/50 sports Panhard-Levassor in single-seater form.

If it is true that the delay in letting loose the big Renault was due to overheating troubles, then they must have been decidedly worried at Billancourt when Bentley Motors brought another 3-litre Bentley to Montlhéry late in March for an attempt on the twenty-four-hour record. Under the control of W O Bentley, the drivers were Barnato, Benjafield, Kensington Moir, and Frank Clement. They drove for three-hour spells. After a delay due to a body defect and then rain, the attempt got going, the idea being to average 100mph for the entire duration. After twelve hours the Bentley was within some 300 yards of the four-seater Renault's record distance but plug trouble had been experienced and, although the world 2000 kilometre record was taken from Renault, after 16hr 21min a broken valve spring was followed by a fractured valve stem and the car had to stop. However, a dozen Class D records were claimed, as well as the world and Class kilometre records. The Bentley, which marque, in any case, held the twenty-four-hour record, averaged 103.47mph for the first hour.

In June the Bentley went out again, in the hands of Clement, Duller, and Barnato. Again, it was unlucky, for heavy rain brought the attempt to an end after 16½ hours, but not before the world twelve-hour record had been raised to 100.92mph, while Class D records from 500 kilometres to 1000 miles were also taken.

Then, in July, the Renault was ready and made history in no uncertain fashion by averaging over 100mph for twenty-four hours for the first time. It ran faultlessly, covering 3589.41 miles (or 318.8 miles more than the Bentley), equal to the straight-line distance from London to Baghdad. The average speed was actually 107.9mph, including all depôt stops, and Garfield, Plessier and Guillon also broke the world and Class A records from 500 miles to 3000 miles, 1000 kilometres to 4000 kilometres, and from six to twenty-four hours, at speeds of from 110.14mph (at six hours) to 107.49mph (for 2000 miles). Demonstrating its true speed, the Renault covered the last lap at 119.2mph (later corrected to

118.74mph). All at Billancourt could breathe freely again!

This magnificent performance by Renault overshadowed a gallant run by Miss Violet Cordery, who, assisted by some mere males in the guise of Moy, Mills, Garland and Byng, drove a 19.6hp Invicta at Montlhéry to break world and Class records from 4000 kilometres to 5000 miles at over 70mph, taking these records from an OM, which established them at Monza. The Invicta was in action for nearly seventy-one hours.

This gained Miss Cordery the Dewar Trophy.

It was unusual for E A D Eldridge to be absent from the Paris track, but he had been busy at Indianapolis. Re-crossing the Atlantic, he arrived at Montlhéry with a Miller single-seater and proceeded to set up new records for five kilometres, five miles and ten kilometres, at speeds from 125.59mph to 121mph. This roused Panhard-Levassor and they sent out Breton in a 7.9-litre sleeve-valve straight-eight. He was able to re-take the world fifty kilometre record at 128.6mph and the fifty mile record at 129.6mph, the Panhard's fastest lap being 133.2mph. Breton then got into the four-cylinder, 5517cc Panhard-Levassor and went even faster, increasing the world five mile record to 138.5mph, and the ten kilometre to the same speed, while the Class D five kilometre record fell at 139.3mph.

Eldridge naturally refused to lie down under this onslaught, and at show time he was out in the Miller in its 2-litre form. He set the five mile record at 140.6mph (in 1926, remember), the ten kilometre record to 140.2mph, and, while going on for ten kilometres, averaged 131.1mph, breaking another Panhard record. Breton's Panhard failed to beat these speeds but set up new Class D figures.

Racing was less intense at Montlhéry in 1926 than in 1925. For one thing, the French Grand Prix was banished to Miramas, where it was singularly unsuccessful, although that's another story. The Grand Prix du Salon was held in October, but rain fell throughout. Alas, the GP Delage cars were withdrawn, enabling the Talbots of Segrave, Divo and Moriceau to dominate the 1500cc category, while the Amilcar Sixes of Morel, Martin and Duray did likewise in the 1100cc class, the official Salmson entries being absentees.

The races were run off in two heats of the short road circuit, followed by a final over the banked circuit, Duray winning the first of these finals at 102mph. All three race times were added together, making Duray's Amilcar the victor from Perrot's Salmson and Sandford's Sandford three-wheeler. Divo won the 1500cc race, his Talbot averaging 62.6mph for sixteen laps of the full road circuit. Segrave was second and Moriceau third, the Talbots easily vanquishing the next car home, Guyot's sleeve-valve Guyot Special, which was three laps in arrears but ahead of the three Jean Gras.

If racing was unspectacular at Montlhéry in 1926, at least the Paris track had seen two notable achievements that season – over 120 miles covered for the first time in sixty minutes and a speed of 100mph exceeded for twenty-four hours.

So far as Montlhéry was concerned, 1926 faded out with a last minute onslaught on Class E records by Ernest Eldridge, who claimed the fifty kilometre, fifty mile and 100 kilometre records with his 2-litre Miller at speeds of 123.9, 124.8 and 125.1mph respectively. Eldridge took these records two days before the end of the old year, depriving Campbell (Bugatti) and Segrave (Sunbeam) of the honours.

Then, on New Year's Eve, Eldridge was out again, his Dunlop-shod Miller this time lifting the 100 kilometre figure to 126.8mph, covering 100 miles at 127.1mph and taking the coveted hour record from Parry Thomas at 126.51mph (all of these were world records).

*Front view of the Panhard-Levassor built for 1500cc record attempts; 1926. (*The Autocar*)*

The Renault 45 which broke the world twenty-four-hour record at 107.9mph in 1926. (Régie Nationale des Usines Renault)

Chapter 4

1927: the year of the Voisin

The 1927 season was enlivened by the announcement of an ambitious Eight-day French Tourist Trophy, a high-speed trial which replaced the Tour de France motoring marathon, in which interest had waned.

Racing began on 13 March, even earlier than usual, starting with the GP de l'Ouverture for cars up to 200cc. The race, over 155 miles, was held on the Sunday on a wet track. The spectators expressed their displeasure when the GP Talbot failed to start, it was said because Divo had an injured hand, although Moriceau was present and wasn't substituted. However, one of the low-slung straight-eight GP Delage cars, driven by Benoist, was there. On the opening lap it ran right away from the field, and would probably have shattered the lap record had the track been dry. Benoist won at 76.3mph after completing one circuit at 79.7mph: we are, of course, talking of the road course. Lescot (1½-litre Bugatti) was left two laps behind and Eyston (2-litre Bugatti) and Esclasson (1½-litre Bugatti) four laps in arrears. Hawkes drove the Eldridge but retired with supercharger trouble.

The 1100cc race was dominated by the Salmsons, de Marnier winning at 67.2mph from Goutte and Perrot over thirty-one miles of the short road course, while Casse's Salmson had made fastest lap at 71.6mph, which seems to have over-cooked its plugs. Goutte then won the next race at 67mph from de Marnier and Perrot.

The Montlhéry organizers obviously loved variety, because the final was moved to the banked track, where de Marnier's Salmson won the 7½-mile sprint at exactly 100mph from Goutte and Perrot. All three cars were Cozette-blown Salmsons.

A match race between Divo's 4-litre vee-twelve Talbot (surely

our old friend the Land Speed Record Sunbeam driven by
Segrave?) and Benoist's big vee-twelve Delage fell through due
to the former's hand injury, Benoist going round carefully in the
rain.

Eldridge presented Benoist with a bouquet, this being the
English driver's first appearance since his accident at Montlhéry
five weeks earlier, when the Miller had crashed in mysterious
circumstances, Eldridge sustaining injuries from which he never
fully recovered. Eldridge had reduced the engine capacity of the
Miller from 2 litres to 1½ litres, and was making a bid for Class F
world records. He had done a few fast laps and came in complaining
that the car wasn't steering properly. A bolt holding the front axle
to a spring was found to be broken, but the axle had not moved.
Whilst this bolt was being replaced, smaller wheels and tyres were
fitted, presumably to lower the gear ratio. Again, Eldridge came in
complaining that the Miller felt odd but, as nothing wrong could
be found, he set off again. He lost control while on the banking,
just beyond the stands, the car snaking then diving down the
banking into the soft infield – where Eldridge was thrown out
onto his head – before rolling over. Among his injuries Eldridge
suffered from dirt and broken glass from his spectacles entering
his eyes, and ever after wore a shade over one of them.

The next excitement seems to have happened just before Easter,
when Marchand broke the Miller's 100 kilometre and 100 mile
records very handsomely. He drove a new straight-eight, sleeve-
valve Voisin, a special racing car sporting a well-streamlined, two-
seater body with flat belly; a cover over the mechanic's seat and
cowlings over the radiator and front dumb-irons, although the
front springs were exposed. The 95 x 140mm (7938cc) engine was
offset in the chassis, and had a very large oil radiator below and
to each side of the crankcase fed by air louvres in the undertray.
Ignition was by Delco coil and dynamo. Two Zenith carburetters
were bolted to the cylinder block on the nearside, an enormous
Y-shaped aluminium air manifold – in turn bolted to the intakes
– bringing the air through a big Tecalemit air filter connected

by flexible tubing to the base of this manifold. This Voisin was low slung, both axles passing above the side members; for the record attempts only a direct drive was used in the gearbox. Discs were used on the back wheels only. The back axle contained a differential. Fuel and oil tanks in the long tail gave 1½ hour's duration; for an hour's run with driver, the start-line weight was 27½cwt. The steering wheel was on the offside with instruments placed at an angle on the left of the cockpit.

Marchand averaged 127.54mph for the 100 kilometres, and knocked thirty seconds off Eldridge's 100-mile record at 128.55mph. Obviously. the 'hour' was Voisin's aim but one rear tyre (they were S S Dunlops on Rudge wire wheels) was observed to be wearing unduly and the car was called in twelve minutes before the hour was up. Some time later Marchand achieved his goal, the Voisin covering 128.35 miles in the hour.

Meanwhile, Eldridge's Miller had been repaired and given to little Douglas Hawkes, who revenged its owner's accident by taking the 1½-litre hour record with it at 113.339mph, the 100-mile class record taken on the way at 113.48mph. A fatal accident had caused Panhard-Levassor to abandon the very slim 1½-litre single seater steered by a hoop round the driver instead of a steering wheel (to lower the driver's seat for better streamlining), which had been built in 1926 expressly to attempt the hour record.

Reverting to the eight-day trial Devaud's Amilcar covered the greatest distance: 3192 miles in eighty hours, inclusive of all stops, over the road circuit. Rigal's 750cc Peugeot was second, averaging 39mph to the Amilcar's just under 40mph. Doré won the 500cc class on a two-stroke Sima-Violet, with 2485 miles.

In this eventful year, when Segrave exceeded 200mph for the first time, the Model A Ford superseded the Model T, and a *Musée des Voitures* was opened in a restored wing of the Château de Compiègne, Montlhéry was the scene of the French Grand Prix.

The day before the French Grand Prix was contested, a free-for-all, or *Formule Libre* race, was held. The seven starters were certainly an astonishingly mixed bag, ranging from the lady driver of a Grand Prix Salmson to two of the 4-litre supercharged vee-twelve Sunbeams in the hands of Louis Wagner and Williams. However, when the pack was released it was Albert Divo's 1½-litre Talbot which accelerated away in the lead, with the two supercharged 2.3-litre Bugattis of Chiron and Eyston behind. The race was held over the road-cum-track circuit which was to be used for the Grand Prix the following day. The cars ran off the banking, past the water tower, along the twisting 1-in-8 descent to Les Bruyères hairpin, up to the Les Biscornes loop, back along the straight to La Forêt corner, through the Couard bends in Bailleau Wood, and so back on to the track proper by way of the left-hand corner by the car park and through Le Fays hairpin. All this proved too much for the three-speed track gearbox of Wagner's Sunbeam, but for ten laps Williams held his big green Sunbeam ahead of the low blue Talbot.

The course was slippery after all-night rain, but Divo opened up on the second lap, which the Talbot covered at a satisfactory average of 71.5mph, and passed the Sunbeam. These two led the Bugattis of Chiron and Eyston, a Guyot Special and Madame Derancourt's Salmson.

Then Williams' Sunbeam went out, also with gearbox failure, the second-speed gears having seized, perhaps to the driver's relief for these cars had proved far too powerful for the road circuit, being prone to tail slides that were not easy to control.

This dull race looked like ending in a procession when, unfortunately, on the fourth lap de Courcelles lost control of the never very stable Burt McCollum-engined Indianapolis Guyot Special. The car left the road at some 100mph, hit a tree and virtually exploded, killing the driver. The accident resulted in an excitable French doctor driving the ambulance against the competitors still in the race, and on the wrong side of the road. Divo cut out and got through, but Chiron was forced to take his Bugatti on round the track instead of turning into the road circuit, running on to the soft infield to pull up. He was able to turn and continue, and the results were:

1st   A Divo (Talbot) 1hr 2min 20½ sec, 74.75mph
2nd   L Chiron (Bugatti) 1hr 2min 5sec
3rd   G E T Eyston (Bugatti)

After this tame 'free-for-all' was the Sporting Commission Cup Race which had brought in entries of two Peugeots, four BNCS, three Bugattis, a four-cylinder, two-stroke Leroi, a Georges-Irat, two Salmsons, three Lombards, a Corre La Licorne, a De Coucy, and two Montiers.

The race was run over 248½ miles on a fuel consumption basis, competitors permitted an allowance of 97lb of fuel and oil, including the oil in the gearbox.

Peugeot decided to build special cars for this queer race, using normal 2.6-litre, 80 x 124mm, sleeve-valve engines with a compression ratio of 7.9:1. The Knight engines, normally regarded as thirsty oil drinkers, were each given only 1¹⁄₁₀ gallons of oil but the Peugeot engineers expected to find at least half a gallon remaining at the finish. This left enough fuel for the cars to run at the rate of 21.73mpg. A very clever contribution to reducing oil use was made by eliminating the gearbox after the cars had started. It was arranged for the layshaft to be immobilized, meaning that only two ball races remained in use and no oil was deemed necessary in the gearbox! To help the limited amount of engine oil in its task, about one-third of the radiator was devoted to cooling this lubricant, and a pump drew off oil from a tank near the bottom of the radiator and fed it to the engine.

These Peugeots had special chassis frames with high thin section girder side members, through which passed both the axles. Springs, shock absorbers, steering connections and exhaust pipe were all within the frame, which was covered by thin sheet aluminium, and the gearbox and propeller shaft was offset to the offside, the driver sitting low down on the left in the single-seater body. Front brakes were dispensed with; these Peugeots weighed only 11cwt 61lb with tanks empty, or 17lb per hp. They were well streamlined, with a headrest behind the driver, and had a wheelbase of 8ft 1in and a track of 4ft. The highest part of the radiator was less than forty inches from the ground. The petrol tank was in the scuttle overhanging the gearbox. It fed initially by gravity and afterwards under pressure, a gauge keeping the driver aware of the contents. Well-base wire wheels were shod with Dunlop tyres.

It is nice to be able to record that these careful preparations brought Peugeot victory in this distinctly odd race. André Boillot drove whilst suffering badly from neuralgia, his face hidden under bandages, and, lapping cautiously to conserve fuel, at 62.63mph. He led all the way until challenged on the very last lap by Doré, whose Salmson opened up at the very end, causing Boillot to increase to 100mph or so and climb the banking for the first time. He won by a mere ⅔ths of a second.

The Lombards had driven off the course when they were found to be unprepared for a race of this length; the second Peugeot proved difficult to start and managed only three-quarters of the distance, and Goutte's Salmson lost second place because its rear petrol tank sagged and prevented petrol reaching the tank on the dash. Superchargers were used by Bugatti and BNC without detrimental effect on fuel economy. The results were:

1st Boillot (Peugeot) 3hr 53min 101sec
2nd Doré (Corre la Licorne) 3hr 53min 211⅔sec
3rd Goux (s/c Bugatti) 3hr 54min 27⅘sec
4th Goutte (Salmson)
5th Conelli (s/c Bugatti)
6th Chase (Salmson)
7th Rost (Georges-Irat)

Storms on the preceding day gave way to fine weather for the French Grand Prix, and the biggest crowd yet seen at Montlhéry — an estimated 100,000 spectators — came to watch the race, which became a battle between the low-hung, supercharged straight-eight Delage and Talbot cars, with the Bugattis outclassed. On

55

the opening lap Divo clocked 6min 6sec (75.15mph), Benoist's Delage being ⅖ of a second behind the leading Talbot, and Williams' Talbot a further ⅖ of a second astern. Divo completed his second lap in 5min 5sec (78.32mph) and the order remained unchanged. Wagner's Talbot had lost time at the start, Eyston's six-cylinder Halford Special was too slow, but behind Williams the Delage cars of Bourlier and Morel were warming to the attack.

Wagner, trying to wipe out his disadvantage, lapped at 78½mph and on the third lap Benoist took the lead, having set a new lap record of fractionally over 79mph. He held this desirable position for the entire race and pushed the lap record ever higher, first to 81.5mph, then to 81.99mph.

The Talbots of Williams and Divo, now in that order, were no match for the Delage and Williams' car was suffering from trouble with the petrol pump. Morel's Delage, which needed to have all four wheels changed, was also having petrol feed problems. Divo slipped back into second place but couldn't do anything about the Delage. Benoist averaged exactly 80mph to quarter distance.

Wagner was pressing Bourlier for third place until his Talbot began to spit back while on the banking. Many of the cars were calling for a change of all wheels, and Bourlier's Delage had all its plugs changed as well as a prearranged pit-stop, and went on to take second place from Divo. The latter's Talbot was soon in real trouble, which a change of plugs did not rectify.

Benoist's pit-stop was spectacular (one of the joys of the race spectator in those days), the Delage skidding to a standstill and the driver and his Italian mechanic working feverishly on it. The car resumed the race in the lead, whereas Divo's Talbot had been retired, probably with valve trouble, after the mechanic had exhausted himself pushing it round in wide circles in front of the pits trying to restart it.

Delages now held the first two places. Wagner was still waiting to strike but was forced to stop on three successive laps, his Talbot running hot because a water hose had become detached. The engine recovered fully, but rather too late. Eventually, however,

Wagner retired, so Morel automatically went up a place, Delages finishing 1st, 2nd and 3rd. The results were:

1st   Benoist (Delage) 4hr 45min 41⅕sec 77.24mph
2nd Bourlier (Delage) 4hr 53min 55⅗sec
3rd   Morel (Delage) 5hr 11min 31⅖sec
4th   Williams/Moriceau (Talbot). Flagged off, 93 miles behind:
Eyston (Halford Special)
Retired: Wagner (Talbot), 43 laps; Divo (Talbot), 23 laps

In August a twenty-four-hour sports car endurance race was held at Montlhéry, very similar to Le Mans, although there were no restrictions on the fuel used and electric starters were not compulsory, nor had hoods to be erected. Thirty-four thousand francs was offered in prize money.

Eighteen cars left the start at 6pm on the Monday, the field comprising the Le Mans 4½-litre Bentley driven by Clement and Duller, three Fastos, a Georges-Irat, two Th Schneiders, two SCAPS (one of which was a 1½-litre straight-eight), a Dorman-engined Jean Gras, two Lombards, a BNC, an RH, Madame Morris' D'Yrsan, an air-cooled SARA and an Amilcar. There had also been a Bugatti, but this withdrew after the parade.

In the jostle of the rolling start the Bentley was pushed from its rightful place at the front of the pack, but was soon ahead, nevertheless, and led throughout. During a pit-stop, the car caught fire, the subsequent repairs causing delay but not enough to prevent it winning easily, covering 161 laps of the full circuit, or 1247.7 miles. The 1100cc BNC was second, having covered 1162.5 miles, and third place went to another 1100cc car, a Lombard, which ran 1116 miles. A Georges-Irat caught fire and eventually retired, while the other Lombard and a Jean Gras had fallen out very early in the race. The class results were:

Over 3000cc
1st   Clement/Duller (Bentley) 161 laps

2000cc: Gros/Barthelemy (Fasto) 140 laps
1500cc: Guibert/Clement (SCAP) 126 laps
1100cc: Doré/Pousse (BNC) 150 laps

As for record-breaking, the big Voisin – still on Dunlop tyres, with Morel assisting Marchand every ninety minutes – took world honours up to six hours at 116.1mph, prior to raising the twenty-four-hour record to the remarkable level of 113.4mph (2724 miles), which made the poppet-valve Renault 45 look rather cautious! Six other world records fell on the way, with Kiritoff – a Voisin export traveller held mainly in reserve – assisting Marchand and Morel. So well did the Dunlop tyres stand up that, instead of changing them at these replenishment stops, the offside rear was changed only every three hours; the nearside was good for 4½ hours but was changed with its fellow, whilst the offside front tyre was replaced every six hours and its companion every 7½ hours. The Voisin had a higher gear ratio than before to reduce rpm from 2600-3000rpm to about 2000rpm. It had cast-iron double sleeve valves and 33 x 5.35in tyres, and ran without lights, aided at night by acetylene searchlights on the track.

Apart from one slight shower the weather was kind to this ambitious and successful record-breaking attempt, which Voisin's Chief Engineer, André Lefebvre, supervised.

Towards the end of 1927, George Eyston, driving a GP Bugatti at Brooklands, broke the Miller's 1½-litre hour record. As far as the Paris track was concerned, the year concluded with a remarkable demonstration of mechanical and human stamina when the Hon Victor Bruce and his wife broke world records up to 15,000 miles with an AC Six under appalling climatic conditions, during which the car inverted on the snow-covered track (the attempt took place in December) after 127 hours 'lappery'. The AC was repaired and, after a loss of 15hr 20min (during which average speed fell from some 76 to 63mph), the intrepid Bruces set out to complete their self-imposed task, J A Joyce flying out to help them. He was a stranger to the track, so practised in a saloon before he began his spell at the wheel of the record-breaking AC, very soon lapping at 86mph.

The AC won through, taking seven world records from 4000 miles (at 78.82mph) to 15,000 miles (at 68.01mph), with only the 25,000 mile record remaining unbroken. The only problems, apart from the crash, had been the slackening-off of a contact-breaker nut, two changes of KLG plugs, the original set going back at the second change, a few routine adjustments to the exhaust tappets after six days' running, and to the Hartford shock absorbers, which were tightened on the order of Mr Bruce and then slackened off to suit his wife! The Dunlop tyres endured for twenty-four to thirty hours, even on the back wheels.

This magnificent British record onslaught was celebrated on 22 December 1927 at the Hotel Cecil in London. The run was remarked upon in England as emphasizing the value of the Paris track, for at Brooklands runs exceeding twelve hours were forbidden, with cars locked away during the night so that the stockbrokers on St George's Hill could rest undisturbed. In any case, the Weybridge course was closed for repairs during the winter.

Mrs Bruce at speed in the AC Six with which she and her husband, the Hon Victor Bruce, set world records of up to 15,000 miles in 1927 in appalling wintery conditions.

*The sleeve-valve, 8-litre Voisin which took the world twenty-four-hour record at over 113mph in 1927. (*The Autocar)

*Left: The AC
Six during
the epic
15,000
miles
record trial.*

*Above: George Duller in the 4½-litre Bentley
during the 1927 Twenty-four hour race.*
(The Autocar)

61

Chapter 5

1928: a mixed bag of record-breakers

The 1928 record-breaking season opened at Montlhéry on 14 February, when D M K Marendaz, aided by Montlhéry resident Douglas Hawkes, took the Class G twenty-four-hour record from a SAM, which ran at Monza, in a very shapely two-seater Marendaz Special.

This was apparently a stripped Anzani-engined sports Marendaz with engine bore reduced to bring it within the 1100cc class limit. The car averaged 58.1mph for the two rounds of the clock, collecting various other class records on the way, such as the twelve-hour record at 54.67mph. Kaye Don was to have helped throughout but a clumsy mechanic drove the car into a petrol pump (can you imagine what Marendaz said?!) and so damaged the back axle that a new half-shaft had to be machined from an old lorry propeller-shaft. Don was left with only two hours in which to drive, after which Douglas Hawkes and Gwenda Stewart helped out. Then the night was rendered horrible by gusty wind and rain squalls; a gearbox defect left only the highest ratio available, and 1½ hours were lost replacing a broken timing chain.

The next excitement was the arrival of the Hispano-Suiza which had been challenged by a Stutz to a twenty-four hour duel at Indianapolis, in America, which it subsequently won hands down. This fine car was tested at 85mph for several laps, the monotony being momentarily dispelled by the brief appearance of a Le Mans Lombard, and by an Amilcar mechanic borrowing one of the supercharged Amilcars when the head tester was absent, promptly overturning it on his second lap.

Prior to all this Mr and Mrs E W Deeley made a successful long distance run at Montlhéry in a Singer Junior (which has quite a vintage history in spite of the scorn with which the VSCC regards these cars) to settle a dispute between husband and wife. So pleased was the Singer Company that it presented Mrs Deeley with a Singer saloon of her own. Her exploit, carried out in December 1927, consisted of driving round and round Montlhéry for six days and nights, during which time the Singer Junior covered 5671 miles in extremely bad weather conditions, at an average speed of 39.39mph, inclusive of 1hr 38min spent refuelling.

Early in 1928 certain claimed records were renounced by the FICM, Walter's Class H Austin three-hour record being disallowed in favour of Gordon England – today anxious to see our railways converted into roads – who, at Montlhéry in 1924, had averaged 79.16mph for this distance in his Austin Seven.

Class H was now enlivened by an excitable team which would bring a Grazide to Montlhéry, accompanied by an ancient Panhard-Levassor which should certainly now be in the Montlhéry Museum, and set records out of reach of Austin and others. For example, early in 1928 they increased the five mile record to 96.57mph, and the ten mile to 96.22mph. Alas, finances ran short just when 100mph was in sight.

Apart from record bids, weekdays at Montlhéry thirty-three years ago were enlivened by routine testing of standard Amilcars, which, in blown form, had to lap at 99-100mph. The racing version was taken round by Martin at 122mph, whilst an old-type Le Mans Chenard-Walcker, and the Le Mans Salmson driven by Goutte, both lapped at 81mph

Another typically French car which took records at Montlhéry about this time was an 1100cc Cozette with a four-cylinder, horizontally-opposed two-stroke engine and two crankshafts, one above and the other below the cylinders, charging by means of a blower instead of crankcase compression, and two eight-cylinder magnetos. It also had a quite remarkable steering gear involving a chain and many spur gears. With a slim single-seater body and fairing over both axles, the Cozette was an impressive little car, with which Prince Ghia Cantacuzino claimed Class G records up to the hour at over 103mph, obviously with something in hand.

At the same time Gwenda Stewart took out the HS (the initials presumably standing for Hawkes-Stewart, although the car was really the 1925 Jappic evolved by Walters in England), and established records in the smallest category, Class J, averaging nearly 71mph for 100 miles.

Renault, although it had abandoned record-breaking, was using Montlhéry to test the new 40hp straight-eight model saloon, which, incidentally, had the radiator in the conventional location; it made many laps averaging 70-75mph.

Then Marchand had a very narrow escape from death when the big racing Voisin got out of control during an onslaught on the fifty-kilometre and fifty-mile records. After twelve laps the offside rear tyre burst and left the rim; the resultant skid pulled off a front tyre as well. This caused the Voisin to charge the outside retaining wall, some fifty yards of which were carried away before the car went through, fortunately where the drop was only about four feet. Marchand remained in the car and was later operated on in hospital for extensive injuries.

This did not deter Morel from lapping at 126mph in the Amilcar, which was being prepared for the Arpalon Speed Trials where it subsequently vanquished the Salmson opposition. The new six-cylinder Citroën, equipped with a low sports two-seater body, was involved in proving trials, including lapping at 60mph.

*The Marendaz Special which took the 1100cc twenty-four-hour record in 1928. (*The Autocar*)*

Morel later let the supercharged Amilcar Six out at Montlhéry, taking Class G records from five kilometres to ten miles inclusive, at between 124.57 and 127.1mph.

Renault continued to use the Autodrome for research purposes, one experiment consisting of towing one straight-eight behind another, round and round at 50mph; which reminds me that I saw Renault doing exactly the same thing at Montlhéry a few years ago, but with a 4CV towing a Renault van.

Another research exercise consisted of making a Mathis average 80mph for twenty-four hours.

Paris Salon activity at the Paris track included a successful attempt by Douglas Hawkes and Mrs Stewart on on the Class

G (1100cc) twelve-hour record), their little Vernon-Derby — a normal fabric-bodied two-seater sports model, except for tuned engine and extra oil tanks — averaging 66.48mph. An Austin Seven disguised as a Rosengart also tried for records, lapping at 77mph but fading out with piston trouble. A front-wheel-drive Brasier — famous name — was out on experimental work. Winter, indeed, showed no slow-up in activity.

Desvaux and Goutte were busy with a single-seater Cozette-supercharged, roller-bearing four-cylinder Lombard that was lapping at about 103mph, and was destined to try for the Class G hour record — they said at Brooklands. Jealous rivals Morel and Casse were equally concerned by going fast, in Amilcar and Salmson respectively. A Genestin with supercharged 1½-litre SCAP engine had got round at 86mph; Hotchkiss was at Montlhéry for long duration tests, and Marendaz and Kaye Don had their sights set on the Class F twenty-four-hour record.

In due course the Marendaz now a three-seater — made its run, but driven by Forrest and Hawkes. They duly took the record from an FN, in spite of fog and the discovery that the spare magneto rotated in the wrong direction. The average speed was just above 59mph, and thus Marendaz held both the 1100cc and 1500cc twenty-four-hour records.

The Lombard was less successful at first, the back axle puncturing the petrol tank at 100mph, but right at the end of 1928 it broke six Class G records, from 200 kilometres to six hours, at speeds of around 94mph, including stops to change a wheel and a sparking plug. The weather for the drivers, Desvaux, Goutte and Hasley, was horrid.

Chapter 6

1929: Mrs Bruce returns to the attack

Montlhéry seemed less active during the winter of 1928-9 than in previous years, yet ere the cold weather had departed from this country, Divo was out on the Paris track with a 3.3-litre Bugatti, and was said to be contemplating world records with a sixteen-cylinder geared-crankshafts Bugatti, Eldridge, recovering his old form, was busy modifying one of those pleasing two-seater Chryslers for an onslaught on Peugeot's Class C twenty-four-hour record. He attached a big sump to the Chrysler's base chamber with air ducts running through it to cool the oil; the place usually occupied by the dickey seat was used for a huge additional fuel tank which gravity-fed the normal rear petrol tank, its filler protruding through the top of what was the dickey seat lid.

To Eldridge's annoyance the French press announced that he was going for the world twenty-four-hour record, which brought a crowd of spectators, who found him merely grappling with fuel feed troubles, the Chrysler lapping at 75mph.

Douglas Hawkes hoped to take records with the previously mentioned Genestin, but was less optimistic after an oil pipe burst, spraying him with lubricant. Finally, Eldridge and Kaye Don achieved their ambition: the Class C twenty-four-hour record was taken at over 71mph. The Chrysler was virtually standard, relying on its own headlamps during the hours of darkness, and the bonnet was sealed throughout, the hood remaining up. The only fault was a faint fuel leak.

Renewed activity was seen at Montlhéry following the Chrysler's successful run. De Rovin, preparing for the Monaco race, had out one of the 1½-litre GP Delage cars, in it lapping at 117mph. Donnet Cars was thought to be interested in the Class G twelve-hour record, and Lombard hoped first to raise this record to over 90mph, but wrecked an engine when a con-rod broke during trial runs. Later, too, de Rovin's Delage mysteriously lost power, although Philip de Rothschild had a Bugatti going well, and Doré was putting in some useful practice in a Licorne.

With a stripped sports Vernon-Derby, Douglas Hawkes and Gwenda Stewart captured the Marendaz Special's 1100cc twenty-four-hour record at 64.32mph, taking the 1000-mile record at 64.88mph and the 2000-kilometre record at 64.31mph on the way. After this Turnbull and Bull earned some criticism for playing at taking records with an Aston Martin and the ex-Eyston 1½-litre Bugatti, being reminded that national prestige was at stake when Englishmen venture farther abroad than Calais with racing cars! At about this time the Le Mans Chryslers were on test at Montlhéry, lapping at 92mph.

Early in 1929 the Montlhéry authorities decided to issue a special badge, awarded to those who had established or broken records on the track; an excellent idea for which some seventy-four drivers qualifed, notably Mrs Gwenda Stewart, Mrs Victor Bruce, and Miss Violet Cordery. Mrs Bruce was in the news at the time, for she was anxious to rob the Chrysler of its twenty-four-hour record and, moreover, intended to drive the two rounds of the clock single-handed: I can imagine few more exhausting drives. She took over to Montlhéry for the purpose a 'Double Twelve' (no 5) 4½-litre Bentley. She succeeded splendidly, covering 2149.68 miles at an average speed of 89.57mph.

After her run S C H Davis stated that he wasn't in favour of these single-handed, one-driver-only runs, although he was thinking of a twenty-four-hour race – Ramponi had just taken an Alfa-Romeo alone through the JCC 'Double Twelve' at Brooklands – rather than a record attempt.

Excellent as this record was, it serves as a reminder that this was an age when it was still possible to break important international class records with a sports car, or even with a touring car, as D M K Marendaz, who had taken records at Brooklands with a Graham-

Paige saloon, demonstrated by taking to Montlhéry a normal touring Graham-Paige. In this car, assisted by Ashby and Forrest, he broke Class B records for 3000, 4000 and 5000 miles and 4000 and 5000 kilometres, the last 1000 kilometres covered at nearly 75mph and the fastest lap timed at 87½)mph, although dirty fuel stopped the run eventually and restricted overall average speed to 62mph. Incidentally, at the dinner celebrating Mrs Bruce's record, it is said that W O Bentley made the first speech of his life – and there have been very few!

By the summer that fine 'actor' Léon Duray had arrived at Montlhéry from America in a fwd Cord saloon, accompanied by a couple of front-drive Millers and a Miller of more normal conception. His arrival was overshadowed by a fatal accident involving Cozette, when he was testing his inqenious little car with an engine enlarged to 1½-litres, with whlch Gwenda Stewart had hoped to break the 1½-litre hour record. No-one saw the car leave the track but it skidded sideways for many yards before doing so.

Mathis came along with a narrow-track single-seater and Marchand, recovered from his accident, was getting ready a twin-six Voisin for an attempt on world honours up to 200 miles. Amidst all this summer activity, Sénéchal had persuaded a Ford, covered in seals, to average nearly 60mph for twenty-four hours but, alas, an engine seizure precluded a non-stop run.

Léon Duray then went to work, going first to that piece of public road at Arpajon which the French were able to close for racing, to attack the ½-litre ss kilometre record with his Packard-Cable Special, then returning to Montlhéry to break records up to ten kilometres with a ½-litre Miller at over 139mph, and up to ten miles at 135.33mph. Duray had considerable tyre trouble, and had to wait until the cool of the evening before making the attempt. (Incidentally, it was this Miller on which the cylinder head of the Type 51 Bugatti is said to have been based.)

The Mathis set out to cover 15,000 miles. Its propeller-shaft broke after forty-seven hours, but not before de Bremond, Pagniez, Falavier and Nicole had lapped at just over 80mph all that time.

The impressive twelve-cylinder Voisin, with its big stub exhausts and drop-nosed bonnet, was present for a 25,000 mile run at 100mph, and Mrs Stewart demonstrated her versatility by averaging 101½mph for an hour in a 996cc, unblown, vee-twin Morgan three-wheeler; a very stout performance by this slim, determined woman.

Marchand and Morel eventually got going in the big Voisin, the most elaborate equipment being laid on to aid them, including the means of heating fresh sump oil, red lamps energized by their own generating plant to light the track, and a doctor in attendance. Unfortunately, the first job of refuelling went wrong and burst the car's fuel tânk, and when the Voisin resumed, it lapped not at 100 but at 95mph.

Better luck attended a 3½-litre Hotchkiss, set to cover 40,000 kilometres in the care of Tchernovsky, de Corvaia, Delgutte and Vasselle. It broke record after record, the 4000 miles at 78.95mph ranking as a world as well as an international Class record. Spurred on by the proximity of the Paris Salon, the Hotchkiss went on and on, covering 15,000 miles at close on 70mph. Voisin dropped their '25,000 at 100' idea and concentrated on just breaking records, which included many world honours, the car averaging just below 90mph for 15,000 kilometres, and continuing for 20,000 kilometres.

Eldridge, never at rest for long, was intent on recapturing the twenty-four-hour record for Chrysler, but also had a single-seater Riley on the stocks, its Speed Model engine having a shortened stroke to bring it into the 750cc class.

The Hotchkiss finally called it a day (or days) after taking or establishing no fewer than thirty-three records. It actually circulated for sixteen days, averaging almost 66mph throughout, which included covering the last third of the distance on five cylinders because a big-end had run. And the car was operated by a team of amateurs. The Voisin, unlucky from the start, finally crashed, its driver receiving a head wound and lucky to escape with his life.

Montlhéry did not close for winter renovations as did Brooklands Track, but these last long distance runs played havoc with its surface. Nor was the usual use of quick-drying cement proving effective, and parts of the track were thickly coated with oil and rubber.

These conditions and shocking weather notwithstanding, Gwenda Stewart and Hawkes took the 1½-litre twenty-four-hour record with a Vernon-Derby which had a six-cylinder engine in a test chassis and quite a crude body. The car averaged 65.38mph in spite of suffering a fire *en route* when an electrical short set alight the auxiliary petrol tank while Mrs Stewart was driving.

Eldridge took a Riley Nine saloon and an MG Midget to Montlhéry while waiting for the Chrysler and 750cc Riley; the saloon Riley actually setting the Class G 1000-mile record at a rousing 65.83mph.

Thomson, of Thomson and Taylor, went over to help drive the Riley but the attempt ended in a very bad smash. Gwenda Stewart, ever restless, now added short distance records in the Morgan to her bag, including five miles at 106.3mph.

After this Montlhéry closed down earlier than usual. A Bentley intended for a record attempt failed to arrive, whilst a Graham-Paige which Marendaz had intended to drive there had an accident in this country and arrived late. However, before 1929 was over, the car managed to take the Class B twenty-four-hour record during appalling conditions of fog and torrential

Mrs Gwenda Stewart (later Gwenda Hawkes).

*The twelve-cylinder Voisin in 1929. It crashed whilst attempting to break long distance records. (*The Autocar*)*

rain, for some time forced to run at a mere 60mph though taking the 2000-mile record at 86.69mph. The car in question was the straight-eight Brooklands two-seater, in which Marendaz was assisted by Veendam and Tulloch; all of whom faced 'impossible' weather conditions.

Chapter 7

1930: Gwenda Stewart and the Derby-Miller

When 1930 dawned, a very large proportion of records had been established at Montlhéry, held by Renault, Panhard-Levassor, Graham-Paige, Voisin, Bentley, Mathis, Hotchkiss, Invicta, Miller, AC, Packard-Cable Special, Vernon-Derby, Amilcar, Cozette, Lombard, Salmson, Riley, Grazide, Austin, de Rovin, and HS.

During 1930 this industrious work continued. Before the Easter Brooklands Meeting had been held in England, Jack Dunfee had journeyed to Montlhéry with a 2-litre Grand Prix Sunbeam, intent on world records. He went out after the 200-mile and 200-kilometre honours held by Kaye Don but, alas, the Sunbeam dropped a valve before going the distance. At least these records still belonged to Sunbeam! Some consolation, perhaps, for the troubles Don was having, out in America, with the 4000hp 'Silver Bullet'.

A successful record onslaught was made at Montlhéry by a 500cc, vertical twin, two-stroke DKW two-seater, completely equipped even to a luggage grid. It broke records from 100 miles to twenty-four hours, at between 68.37mph and 56.86mph, mopping up all class records on the way; a fine achievement by this unconventional German car and its drivers, Baron Koenig, von Fachsenfeld, and F C Meyer.

Then 'Tim' Birken had been to the Paris track with the supercharged 4½-litre Bentley single-seater, lapping at 138mph but unable to try for the hour record (Voisin, 128.35mph) because no time-keepers were available; they were all in Morocco to see a team of straight-eight Renaults win the sports car race.

As summer approached Gregoire, the front-wheel-drive

exponent, was testing a Le Mans Tracta at Montlhéry. Gwenda Stewart and S C H Davis were busy with a 1100cc Morgan three-wheeler, which, after a piston had broken and a new air-cooled vee-twin engine had been substituted, took the twelve-hour record at 72.72mph, the 1500-kilometre record at 116.813kph, the 2000-kilometre record at 115.541kph, the 1500-mile record at 71.53mph, the 2500 kilometre at 71.66mph, and the twenty-four-hour record, after stopping after twenty-one hours, at 64.85mph.

Next, it was the turn of the irrepressible Eldridge, who, with George Eyston, took a Riley Nine 'Monaco' saloon to Montlhéry, and, after having the bonnet sealed, claimed the Class G 1000-mile record at 67.79mph before the crankshaft gave up, so robbing them of their hoped-for twenty-four-hour record.

The Riley had a big fuel reservoir in the luggage boot, two Tecalemit petrol pumps to cope with the increased supply, and a reserve water tank.

From record breaking to racing, Montlhéry held its fourth Women's Day in May, all races for the fair sex. To provide a basis for a handicap, drivers of the calibre of Wagner and Bourlier drove the ladies' cars the previous day, but were slower than the owners, out of respect, perhaps, for cars that were not their own. As a reminder that Paris wasn't far away there was an open-air dancing exhibition and an elegance competition. In the races one car overturned and another lost a wheel, though fortunately no-one was hurt. The champion was Countess de Lesguesn, driving a two-stroke Sima Standard, while Mlle Maison Rogée won the Feminine Grand Prix in a BNC. Later, a similar meeting was held for actresses.

The Eldridge/Eyston Riley was repaired and took Class G records up to 5000 kilometres, the drivers doing four-hour shifts and getting, also, eight class records, the twenty-four-hour at 66.62mph, and the forty-eight-hour at 64.36mph. As before, the bonnet was sealed, oil being replenished through an external filler and the car carrying extra fuel and water, plus a second battery.

In the summer of 1930 there was a lull in activity at Montlhéry, but Gwenda Stewart took out the air-cooled 1100cc Morgan three-wheeler and set the class record at a very creditable 113.52mph. Her partner, Douglas Hawkes, was busy trying to get a Miller he had brought back from America through French customs.

Eventually, the Miller came to Montlhéry and the intrepid Gwenda broke the 1½-litre 100-mile, one-hour and 200-kilometre records with it, on a gusty day when the car couldn't be fully extended, at – respectively – 118.13, 118.29 and 118.32mph. After this Mrs Stewart drove the Miller in the Arpajon Speed Trials. She got up to some 140mph when the engine 'blew up' in a big way; a costly business which must have made Hawkes very glad he had brought spares over as well as the cars.

Then, one cold, wet, windy early morning in October, Mrs Stewart came out in the rechristened Derby-Miller, now with an enlarged engine which took it into the 2-litre class. In spite of furious wheelspin, she took the class kilometre record at 129.01mph and the five miles at 128.14mph: a foretaste of things to come ...

With the Paris Salon looming, Voisin commenced a long duration run with a twelve-cylinder saloon, using special pit equipment. Driven by Marchand and his brother and Van Voor Ninck, the Voisin ran for eighteen days, claiming the 30,000-mile record previously held by Studebaker, at 74mph.

Missing Brooklands (now closed for winter repairs), owing to tyre trouble, Dudley Froy took an old Le Mans 4½-litre Bentley, no 9, to Montlhéry and, with Jack Field, used this sports car to take five-litre class records for 2000 miles, 2000 kilometres, 3000 kilometres, twelve hours and twenty-four hours, the latter at 91.5mph. Rain, gales and mist were encountered in plenty and, at night, relying only on the Bentley's headlamps, the drivers had a very stiff task, the car sliding around on a number of occasions.

Right at the end of the year activity returned to Montlhéry. Apart from the Bentley's splendid run, S A Payn, Rose-Richards and Scott took a Grand Prix Delage out after the Class F twenty-four-hour record. First, the magneto mounting came adrift, then

Payn had the steering wheel come off the column and the car had to be returned to the depôt by winding it along on the starting handle. Nearly six hours were lost but, in the end, in spite of tackling the dark hours at around 100mph with just a spotlamp lit from an accumulator, and red lanterns round the track, the Delage took the record at 66.89mph, and the 2000 mile and 3000 kilometre class records into the bargain, at 69mph and 68.35mph respectively.

Jack Dunfee – having bored out the engine of the Grand Prix 2-litre Sunbeam so that it just qualified for the 3-litre class, took the five-kilometre record at 126.98mph; the five-mile record at 126.85mph; the ten-mile record at 126.48mph, and the fifty-kilometre record at 117.52mph. Marendaz then took the Class B 200-mile record in frightful weather at 101.86mph in the straight-eight Graham-Paige: later, Veendam 'lost' the car low down on the west banking and crashed through the inner guard rail, badly damaging the car but escaping injury.

Early in 1931 confirmation arrived that Gwenda Stewart had taken the world ten-mile record at Montlhéry, at no less than 137.205mph. This was a very high speed, bearing in mind that the car had a capacity of under 2 litres. It was the second fastest officially timed record of 1930, only fractionally slower than Kaye Don's Brooklands lap record with the 4-litre vee-twelve Sunbeam.

Right at the end of the 1930 season Mrs Stewart again brought out the Derby-Miller to try for the world hour record. A 40mph gale was gusting about the Paris track, and, after a truly hectic drive of fifty miles at an average speed of over 128mph, the slim single-seater swerving horribly as it was caught by the wind coming off the bankings, Douglas Hawkes was obliged to call Gwenda in, because both front tyres – on the driving wheels – were through to the canvas.

The world 100-kilometre record fell, however, at 128.06mph. Gwenda climbed from the narrow cockpit extremely exhausted, but happy in the knowledge that the straight-eight engine would

Mrs Stewart at speed in the Derby Special. (The Autocar)

The 5-litre Graham Paige of Marendaz in 1930.
(The Autocar)

run at a trifle over 8000rpm; the set limit in America at the time for similar engines was 9000rpm. This latter record, although broken in 1930, really counts for the year 1931, as it was not confirmed and on the books until the new year. The same applies to records taken at Montlhéry by George Eyston's astonishing MG Midget on the last day of 1930 when, after waiting days for the weather to improve, he took out Ex 120, the single-seater in non-supercharged form, and broke the Austin's Class H records for 50-kilometres at 86.38mph; for 50-miles at 87.11mph, and for 100-kilometres at 87.3mph, beating Sammy Davis' speeds by some 3mph. A valve then broke and put a stop to the attempt, but Eyston now knew what the little MG should be capable of if supercharged. The chassis was left at Montlhéry and the power unit of Ex 120 sent back to England for this important modification to be carried out.

Chapter 8

1931: George Eyston's remarkable vanishing act

1931 opened with new rules relating to long distance record attempts, which stated that, for record attempts of over twenty-four hours' duration, repairs had to be done with tools and spares carried on the car. Major components such as cylinder blocks, pistons, connecting rods, crankshafts, crank-cases, gearboxes, the gears within the gearbox, and front and back axles must not be changed throughout the timed run. This signalled the end of huge organized repair depôts beside the track and cannibalization of other cars for the sustenance of the record-breaker.

There was, as well, a cloud casting a slight shadow over the future of the Montlhery Autodrome, with ownership being in some doubt. But as we now know, it was Brooklands that went under in the end, not Montlhéry.

Meanwhile, Mrs Gwenda Stewart had come over to England for the British Racing Drivers' Club dinner, where she was presented with a cigarette case in appreciation of her fine record attempts at the French track. She made a speech, awarding credit to her mechanics and *équipe* generally.

The weather in the early part of 1931 precluded serious record-breaking, but George Eyston, aided by Eldridge and Brewster, undertook a twenty-four hour run in torrential rain and a hurricane, using a Singer Ten saloon with sealed bonnet, which managed to average 50.7mph.

John Cobb had had the fuel tank of the big 10½-litre vee-twelve Delage altered, with the idea of using the old car to challenge the hour record. He took it to Montlhéry, after being delayed at French customs, where the car and its special National Benzole fuel were temporarily impounded.

Then Eyston's MG engine — now Powerplus-supercharged

— was built up at Abingdon and, the blower thoroughly tested, was rushed back to Montlhéry where Eyston hoped to be the first driver to exceed 100mph in a 750cc car, before Malcolm Campbell achieved this goal with the Austin Seven at Daytona Beach. An experimental MG 'Tigress' chassis was loaded with the racing engine, a spare engine, and many other parts, and Jackson and Kindell drove in this from England to the depôt MG was using under the Montlhéry banking.

For some time ice prevented Eyston from taking out the car, and then there was trouble with the alcohol fuel due to prevailing cold conditions. Moreover, Campbell, having raised the World Land Speed Record to 246mph, concentrated on the little Austin Seven, which lifted the Class H flying mile record to 94.03mph. At Montlhéry it was not possible to run a two-way mile, so Eyston was further handicapped by having to try and beat the Austin's speed over five miles. The engine gave trouble; before the spare engine could be used, the supercharger gearing had to be altered and other jobs carried out.

Jackson and Kindell laboured in the cold for 106 hours before, on 9 February, 1931, Eyston was able to go out again. Ex 120 began its run in a high wind and drizzling rain, but George Eyston kept his foot down and the MG took four Class H records; five kilometres at 97.07mph, ten kilometres, five miles and ten miles, the latter at 96.91mph. This beat the Austin and Grazide figures but fell short of the hoped-for century.

Extra help for the overworked MG mechanics was rushed out from England, the little power unit checked over, and an arrangement worked out for feeding warm air from around the radiator to the carburetter air intake.

During the last night before the new attempt on the Monday, with crude tools Jackson and Kindell fashioned a cowl for the radiator on the shed floor. Eyston wanted to start his ten mile run — in this now stark but businesslike MG — at 4pm, but the timekeepers' car was involved in an accident on the way to the track and the scene could not be set until dusk of this cold and wet

February evening. A hailstorm caused further delay, but Eyston did a couple of warm-up laps after it abated. He then crossed the timing strip at 6500rpm, equal to just over 100mph, and opened the throttle wide.

On the slippery course Eyston needed to concentrate hard, but falling pressure in the fuel tank made it necessary for him to work the hand-pump and steer with his other hand, the little MG snaking viciously but staying on the track, the revolution counter going on to indicate a steady 7000rpm. A board bearing the figures '103' told Eyston that his ambition was realized: he had exceeded 100mph in a 750cc motorcar for the first time ever. In fact, the MG Ex 120 had taken the Class H five-kilometre record at 103.13mph; the five-miles at 102.76mph; the ten-kilometres at 102.43mph, and the ten-miles at 101.86mph.

It is pleasing to record that, at a luncheon held to celebrate this historic feat, Captain Arthur Waite of the Austin Motor Company attended and, without bitterness, toasted the team which had wrested the honour from his company.

Cobb had no luck, the cold weather disagreeing with the big Delage, which had to return to the UK without having broken any records. Eyston, on the other hand, badly wanted to challenge shorter records with the MG, but snow covered Montlhéry and he had to call off the idea, although he did notch up the MG to better than 97mph at Brooklands.

He then returned to Montlhéry with Albert Denly to try for records with a new four-cylinder, four-carburetter Riley Speed Model painted bright red, with a fairing behind the driver's head. Alas, this new-type Riley had not gone very far, lapping at 105mph, before the crankshaft broke in the most devastating manner.

Gwenda Stewart, naturally, couldn't rest for long and brought out the Derby-Miller, which annexed the Class E ten-kilometre record at 139.80mph; the five-miles at 139.48mph, and the ten-kilometres at 140.47mph. The latter record smashed that taken previously by Varzi's Alfa-Romeo on the road at Cremona at 138.51mph; in the course of its run the 2-litre Derby-Miller lapped at 141.36mph, ⅘ths of a second under the lap record; electrically timed, too.

Dudley Froy then took a 4½-litre Bentley to Montlhéry and, with the experienced Gwenda Stewart to help him – proving she was just as accomplished at driving big rear-drive cars as smaller front-wheel drive versions – established Class B records, raising those for twelve-hours to 97.80mph; the 2000-kilometres to 98.02mph; the 3000-kilometres to 96.96mph; the 2000-miles to 96.67mph, and the twenty-four-hour to 93.42mph (a record already held by the Bentley), as well as breaking the 1000-mile record at 97.75mph. The car was actually owned by the Hon Richard Norton, as referred to in his book *Silver Spoon*, and he and C E Raphael drove as well as Froy and Gwenda Stewart.

Incidentally, it was at this time that André Lagache was having fun beating up larger cars in one of the 'tank'-bodied 1100cc Chenard-Walckers, rendered potent because it had under its wide bonnet a Panhard-Levassor engine taken from one of the Montlhéry record cars: a foretaste of today's highly-tuned Mini-Minors, Sprites, and so forth, which spring similar surprises on unsuspecting drivers of standard models.

The tireless Gwenda then brought out the Derby-Miller for an attempt on the coveted world hour record, but, although the once significant problem of getting the tyres to hold out had been overcome, and the driver broke her own world 100-kilometre record at 128.09mph after forty minutes of steady, very fast lapping, the wretched magneto gave up the ghost.

Gwenda Stewart, however, never gave up, and naturally was soon out again. She had to start on tyres which had already covered sixty-five laps because fresh ones had not arrived at Montlhéry, so she waited until the cool of the evening, and had part of the track watered with a hose, a dodge Parry Thomas had adopted at Brooklands in an attempt to humour the tyres of the Leyland-Thomas. Alas, the Derby-Miller, after running splendidly for twenty laps, pulling a very high final-drive ratio, was ordered to throttle back to 130mph, which oiled a plug!

*A general view of the road circuit during the French Grand
Prix of 1931. (*The Autocar*)*

Montlhéry now had a rest from record-breaking while the
1931 French Grand Prix was contested. This race — unlike the
milk-and-water major races of the present day — was of ten hours'
duration, starting at 8 o'clock in the morning. It attracted the
biggest crowd of spectators ever seen up to this time at Montlhéry
or, indeed, at any race meeting in France.

On a delightful morning in June, at the beginning of the
Parisian *Grande Semaine*, the crowds bestirred themselves as
early as 5am, and vehicles of every kind began to flow out of the
city along the roads leading to Montlhéry, two hours before the

The French Grand Prix of 1931: Ferranti's old Targa Florio Peugeot leads Dreyfus' Maserati. (The Autocar)

Campari (centre) after finishing in second place in the 1931 Grand prix. (The Autocar)

yellow starting flag was due to fall. This display of enthusiasm on the part of the spectators was not without its humorous aspect, because the motor coach conveying the gatekeepers and cashiers to the track developed mechanical derangements, so that the earliest arrivals parked where they liked and went in free of charge. It has been estimated that the 'gate' that day was worth £10,000 and that some £500 was lost on these first arrivals.

Certainly an exciting race was expected, because Alfa-Romeo had sent a team of three of the latest 2.3-litre straight-eights; Bugatti had replied with a team of his new twin-cam 2.3-litre straight-eights, and Maserati also had an entry of three new cars, also straight-eights. True, Ettore Bugatti, shocked by the failure of the Michelin tyres on his heavy 4.9-litre cars at Le Mans the week before, had considered withdrawing his team, but Dunlop covers were flown over from England and expatriate Englishman, Williams, who supplied some from his stock for tests, got a place in the Bugatti team. The official works teams thus comprised Chiron and Varzi, Divo and Bouriat, Conelli and Williams in Bugattis; Campari and Borzacchini, Nuvolari and Minozzi, and Minoia and Zehender in Alfa-Romeos, and Biondetti and Parenti, Dreyfus and Ghersi, and Fagioli in Maseratis. In addition, Mercédès had a semi-official team of 38/250 cars consisting of Caracciola and Merz with an SSKL, and Stofel and Ivanowsky on the stripped Le Mans SSK sports car with a very high axle ratio.

English drivers were paying considerable attention to the French Grand Prix, Sir Henry Birkin entering his 2½-litre Maserati, with George Eyston as co-driver. Earl Howe and the Hon Brian Lewis drove the former's Type 51 Bugatti; Dunfee and Appleyard entered a 1924 GP Sunbeam, and W B Scott and S A Payn a Delage. There were also independents like Sénéchal with a 1926 straight-eight 1½-litre Delage (the actual car Chiron had taken to Indianapolis in 1929), and Ferranti with an ancient Targa Florio Peugeot.

The old GP Sunbeam did not get very far, breaking a transmission universal joint soon after the start, but the leaders set a cracking pace from the outset. Fagioli's Maserati led for three laps, closely pursued by Chiron's Bugatti, the average speed already at better than 80mph with the Italian driver setting a lap speed of 82.47mph on his second lap. Williams then lapped at 84.34mph on his third lap, after passing Biondetti in third place, and Chiron went even faster on his fourth circuit to take the lead from Fagioli. These two drivers, French and Italian, fought a ding-dong duel, during which Fagioli set the fastest lap of the race (which was, of course, over the full road course) at 85mph and re-took the lead.

After an hour Fagioli still led, having covered 82¾ miles; Chiron was second and Maserati third. Three blue Bugattis – driven by Divo, Williams and Lehoux – came next, followed by the Alfa-Romeos of Campari and Nuvolari, then Sénéchal's low, dark blue Delage. The Englishmen were still going, too: Birkin fourteenth; Earl Howe sixteenth, and Scott twentieth.

Already, after just 1½ hours' racing, Ivanowsky brought in his big Mercédès; after the back axle had been examined it was withdrawn. With two hours gone Chiron led by a few hundred yards from Fagioli; blue car versus red. Birkin had come up to tenth place. During the third hour Nuvolari passed Divo and occupied fourth place, but the fastest of the Bugattis, now driven by Varzi, was still comfortably in the lead, four minutes ahead of Fagioli's Maserati.

As time wore on retirements began to thin the field. The second Mercédès lost the use of the clutch, which enabled the driver to disengage the supercharger; the German car was soon brought in and left on the grass verge. Fagioli, relentlessly chasing Varzi's Bugatti, had showers of sparks emanating from the Maserati's brake drum on the front nearside wheel, the spring holding the shoes together having broken. The shoes were fouling the side of the drum and, at the pits, the mechanics decided that nothing could be done to keep the fast Maserati in the race. Bugatti speed was now allied to efficient pit work to give the Molsheim marque a decided superiority. When the alloy-spoke wheels were removed the brake drums came away with them and worn brake shoes could, if necessary, be replaced. Thus, while the Alfa-Romeos were delayed for front brake drums and shoes to be changed, the Bugattis were on their way.

The Chiron/Varzi Bugatti led by six minutes after Fagioli had dropped out, and Divo had his in second place. At half-duration these two 2.3 Bugattis still led, and for a time Williams' 'works' car had been third, until the bolts sheared on the universal joint, allowing Nuvolari – whose Alfa-Romeo had caught Dreyfus' Maserati – to take third place.

After half-duration the toll increased. Wimille's Type 51 Bugatti went out with a broken radius rod; the Eminente/Bourlier Bugatti caught fire and was burnt out because the fuel tank sprang a leak (how many Bugattis have perished in this way?), and Dreyfus had to watch mechanics remove a brake drum from Fagioli's retired Maserati and transfer it to his car. Montlhéry's sinuous road circuit, with its many different corners and changes of surface, was proving hard on the Grand Prix cars of 1931.

Alfa-Romeo was also suffering from severe brake troubles, the Italian mechanics adjusting brakes on a spare front axle in the trench-like pits, preparatory to putting completely new brakes on the front wheels of two of their cars.

At seven hours the Chiron/Varzi Bugatti still led, as it had done since the second hour. The Divo/Bouriat Bugatti was second, Nuvolari kept alive Alfa-Romeo hopes by holding his third place, and Dreyfus (Maserati) was fourth. Minoia (Alfa-Romeo) was fifth and Birkin (Maserati) sixth, with only thirteen cars still running. Then the luckless Tazio Nuvolari became a victim of the all-too-prevalent brake trouble, which dropped him to fifth place after eight hours, Campari's Romeo moving up to third place and the Birkin/Eyston Maserati to fourth.

Earl Howe was in trouble in the early evening with a mysterious misfiring on his Bugatti, which was in and out of the pits until eventually a faulty insulation on an HT cable was discovered where it was hidden inside the metal conduit.

The drivers, as well as the cars, now began to show signs of

George Eyston in the MG which was the first 750cc car to attain 100mph in 1931. E A D Eldridge (in hat and coat) stands behind the car). (The Autocar)

strain, for hands were torn and backs stripped of skin after hours of driving round the Montlhéry road course. So slippery were the corners that the cars were sliding wildly, and passing was prudent only on the straights. Even so, the end of this long road race was quite dramatic.

Birkin was pressing Campari hard, hoping that his rival's brakes would give out and enable the cars to change places. Then, a mere thirty-five minutes from the finish, Divo stopped because the engine bolts of his Bugatti had worked loose and, with no tools on the car, he was helpless and unable to continue. Varzi was at once signalled to slow down, and did so, but on his final lap he speeded up his Dunlop-shod, KLG-equipped Bugatti to equal his previous best lap. He then went on for an additional lap to make quite certain of victory for France, the blue car being the last to finish. Twelve cars completed the course out of twenty-three starters, the Divo/Bouriat Bugatti placed seventh on distance covered, even though it had retired! Sénéchal drove alone all the way and did well to get the 1½-litre Delage home in fifth place. The results were:

1st   Chiron/Varzi (Bugatti) 78.1 miles 78.16mph

*George Eyston (in cockpit) and E A D Eldridge (in hat) with the unsupercharged Riley Nine that averaged 108.11mph for an hour in 1931. (*The Autocar*)*

2nd   Campari/Borzacchini (Alfa-Romeo) 755 miles
      75.50mph
3rd   Biondetti/Parenti (Maserati) 737 miles 73.73mph
4th   Birkin/Eyston (Maserati) 736.7 miles 73.68mph
5th   Sénéchal (Delage) 710 miles 70.90mph
6th   Minoia/Zehender (Alfa-Romeo) 699.9 miles 69.96mph
7th   Divo/Bouriat (Bugatti) 699 miles 69.89mph
8th   Dreyfus/Ghersi (Maserati) 688 miles 68.85mph
9th   Rigal/Ferranti (Peugeot) 665 miles 66.52mph
10th Pesato/Felix (Alfa-Romeo) 656 miles 65.62mph
11th Nuvolari/Minozzi (Alfa-Romeo) 652 miles 65.24mph
12th Howe/Lewis (Bugatti) 606.4 miles 60.64mph

The whole of the outer circuit now being available again, Gwenda Stewart brought out the Derby-Miller once more for her attempt on the world hour record. She was again unfortunate, for the standing-start lap was seven seconds down due to a worn gear pinion, which Douglas Hawkes had not thought it worth replacing, causing the gear lever to go into neutral at anything over 2500rpm; yet another example of how, in motor racing, nothing can ever be left to chance, reflecting credit on this very experienced lady driver, inasmuch as she did not let the engine over-rev in the clrcumstances.

Indeed, she pressed on so well that after eight laps she had recovered the time lost, and after twenty-four laps had been completed she had eight seconds in hand over the self-imposed schedule. This the slim Derby-Miller kept up for forty-four laps, or rather over half way, when severe engine trouble intervened. However, the world 100-kilometre record was taken at 128.16mph, and Class records for fifty-kilometres (126.81mph) and fifty-miles (127.97mph) fell as well.

Ettore Bugatti had issued a free-for-all challenge, with prize money amounting to 300,000 francs, in a five-day race at Montlhéry for cars in racing trim, the rules insisting that cars should be locked up overnight. Bugatti had decided after Rost's accident at Le Mans that touring equipment on racing cars added to the hazards, as did racing after dark.

Gwenda Stewart brought the Derby-Miller to Brooklands for the August Bank Holiday Meeting, but the engine had had to be hastily rebuilt after the calamity during the hour record attempt, and the patched-up crankcase split from end to end. Her best Brooklands lap was at 116.84mph on this occasion.

George Eyston obviously had to have another go at record-breaking before long, and this he did with a Phoenix Park-type, four-carburetter Riley Nine, which used a well-streamlined body with headrest, and an ingenious external exhaust system whereby four separate pipes merged to twin tail pipes immediately aft of the cockpit. George, with Eldridge in attendance, drove extremely consistently, taking the Class G hour record at 108.11mph, the 200-kilometre at 108.28mph, and the fifty-kilometre, fifty-mile, 100-kilometre and 100-mile Class records *en route*, all at over 108mph (these records were previously held by Staniland's linered-down blown Bugatti and the Cozette Special).

Late in the summer of 1931 there should have been record attempts at Arpajon and Montlhéry, but neither received enough support. However, on lone record sorties the 100mph Austin, two MGs and a Riley were availing themselves of the Paris track. Gwenda Stewart batted first, with the 'Dutch-clog'-type Austin Seven (side fuel tanks making the car reminiscent of Segrave's 'Golden Arrow') and did 109.13mph for five kilometres, 109.06mph for five miles, and 108.95mph for ten miles. Eyston, with little Albert Denly, was, for the time being, concerned with more Class G records, of which the unsupercharged Riley Nine took the 200-mile record at 104.19mph, the 500-kilometres at 104.08mph, the three-hours and the 500-mile record at 98.18mph, in spite of having to avoid wreckage strewn about the track when a motorcycle ran into the back of a car. Later, Eyston took the Class G six-hour record at 99.06mph, and the 1000 kilometres at 99.24mph.

Next, it was Mrs Stewart's turn again. She and the little Austin Seven took the Class H fifty-kilometre record at 98.09mph and the fifty-miles at 98.43mph before the crankshaft objected. This run was primarily undertaken to glean information for the forthcoming BRDC 500 Mile Race at Brooklands. As a result, the fuel tanks were removed from the sides of the car and placed under the scuttle, and the tail cut down.

Eyston now had the new single-seater MG Midget, Ex 127, ready for an attempt on the short distance Class H records.

An MG had been the first 750cc car officially to reach 100mph, and naturally the Abingdon-on-Thames company was very anxious to beat Austin to the first 100-miles-in-the-hour with a 750cc car. So Ex 127 and the older Ex 120 MG were sent to Montlhéry, the former on a lorry, and 'Jacko' Jackson driving the latter. After the yellow Austin Seven had run into trouble and been sent back to England the MG *équipe* remained alone at Montlhéry. Twenty-four hours later Eyston decided to go out in Ex 120 and try for the hour record. George is a big, well-built man and he had literally to be wormed into the narrow cockpit of the little MG, which was restricted by long-range tanks. Settled in, he did three laps at 102mph, came in, pronounced himself satisfied, and set off in an attempt to be the first driver in the world to cover over 100 miles in an hour in a baby racing car. The date was 25 September, 1931.

The standing-start lap was covered at 94mph, and soon the little MG was circulating Montlhéry at over 100mph. This continued for fifty-eight out of the sixty minutes, when the engine began to misfire. Eyston had feared high oil temperature, for the day was close and warm. This did not materialize, but he *was* troubled by having to operate the air pressure pump for the fuel feed at frequent intervals. The misfiring cured itself, the MG went on its way, and the Class H hour record fell at 101.1mph – the methodical Eyston and his MG had achieved their target.

Alas, he decided to cover one more lap to make quite certain he had been going for a full hour, and, with the tiny engine still running at over 6800rpm, the MG disappeared out of the sight of the jubilant onlookers at the depôt. It never reappeared. Hearing the exhaust note cut out abruptly, Jackson and Marney rushed to a car and drove round the track to where the MG was rammed against the earth bank at the side of the course, burning furiously. They jumped from their car and ran to the wreckage, believing, naturally, that Eyston was trapped in the narrow cockpit, into which they had with considerable difficulty inserted him just over an hour earlier. Only when they had bravely kicked in the side of the body did they discover that Eyston wasn't in the car. Now, choked by the acrid smoke and Marney badly burned, the two men searched the deserted track for their driver. But all trace of George Eyston had vanished. Even when help arrived, no-one could solve this ghastly problem.

In fact, Eyston had suddenly found himself enveloped in flames when a petrol pipe union had given way and blazing fuel had flooded the bottom of the cockpit. By a miracle he had managed to get out of his seat and, steering the car to the infield at 100mph, waited until the heat became unbearable, then threw himself out as the MG was still doing 60mph. He landed on soft earth and lay there until the driver of a Citroën that was using the track at the time came upon the scene, lifted Eyston's thirteen stone over his shoulder, dumped him in the Citroën and rushed Eyston to the first aid post. Thus it was that no trace of the driver was found when his helpers arrived! Eyston was badly burned but cheerful when told he had broken the hour record at over 100mph before his accident.

In fact, he had also taken the Class H fifty-kilometre record at 98.7mph, the fifty-miles at 99.8mph, the 100-kilometres at 100.3mph and the 100-miles at 100.09mph, besides the coveted hour record at 101.1mph,

Eyston was taken to a hospital in Paris, and the MG *équipe* turned its attention to Ex 127. On test Denly had discovered that the new single-seater would cover only two laps before boiling occurred. Modifications were made to the cowllngs, but the real trouble was restriction of airflow to the radiator by the bigger supercharger used on this car. Cecil Kimber of MG consulted

Eyston in Paris and it was agreed to fit an aircraft-type surface radiator. This proved effective and on 31 September Eldridge — driving for the first time in a really fast car since his crash in the Miller — captured the Class H five-kilometre record from Austin at 110.28mph, before the head gasket blew and some of the radiator tubes burst, sending scalding water back over the driver's feet. The car was returned to England for a smaller blower to be substituted, so that the original radiator could be reinstalled. By the time this was done Brooklands had closed for winter repairs, but Eyston, rising from his sick bed, instructed MG to return the car to Montlhéry. Denly and Jackson tested Ex 127 and notified Eyston that all was working properly. He and Eldridge then left London for Paris on 21 December, but were told by Jackson not to bother to present themselves at Montlhéry the following day because the track was covered in ice. Eyston, who had not driven a fast car since his accident, merely ordered that the straights be swept where they merged with the high bankings and set out for the track.

Over patches of ice, in a biting wind, Eyston set off to wind-up the narrow green MG. He was quite fearless and it was his helpers who were anxious. All went well, however, and the five-kilometre record was raised to 114.77mph, the fastest Class H record on the books. Eyston went on to take the five- mile record at 114.74mph, the ten-kilometre record at 114.72mph, and the ten-mile record at 114.46mph. After this he called it a day; it was 1932 before he achieved his goal of two-miles-a-minute.

A result of Eyston's crash at Montlhéry in 1931 was that his famous asbestos overalls came into being, and probably ever after meant that scrutineers paid particular attention to fireproof bulkheads between the engine and cockpit of racing cars.

The latter part of the 1931 Montlhéry season had thus been occupied with MG record-breaking activities which were both dramatic and successful.

Meanwhile, Sénéchal and Ferret had used the Delage for a twenty-four-hour record challenge in Class C, succeeding only by a small margin because an hour was lost whilst swarms of mechanics repaired a leaking radiator. The attempt had been unusual inasmuch as Sénéchal lapped at 108mph very high up the bankings, whereas Ferret, during his spells, held the Delage on the fifty foot line.

The engine of the Derby-Miller was properly rebuilt by the tireless Douglas Hawkes, and Gwenda Stewart was able to lift the world 200-kilometre record to 121.75mph, taking, additionally, the Class E 100-mile record at 121.64mph and one-hour record at 121.7:3mph. Then Maurice Benoist and Zehender had a turn at record-breaking with an Alfa-Romeo, taking the Class E 500-mile record at 97.98mph; the 1000-mile at 97.40mph; the 1000-kilometre at 156.283mph, and the six-hours at 96.85mph. These records were established for an oil company. Another oil company had a Peugeot driven round for five hours *sans* radiator or water to demonstrate the effectiveness of its lubricant!

*Eyston proceeds more sedately on a twenty-four hour run with a 10hp Singer. (*The Autocar*)*

End-of-season records included the Class J (350cc) 200-kilometres at 63.29mph, and three-hours at 50.21mph taken by a diminutive Voran, while Marchand, Fortin, Delepine and Gombette finally brought their Citroën to rest, having broken half a dozen Class D records and established eight more, including nine days' driving, using the car's own headlamps at night, at 67.30mph. The Voran then got the Class 1 (500cc) fifty-mile and 100-kilometre records, the former at 77.31mph.

At Paris Motor Show time, Gwenda Stewart was awarded — deservedly — the Montlhéry Challenge Trophy for her splendid and courageous world record attempts with the Derby-Miller, which was by now more Derby than Miller. In addition, she had established some highly creditable records with a Morgan three-wheeler, in which she managed, by sheer determination, to establish several records on a snow-covered track, the fastest being fifty kilometres at no less than 105mph.

Mrs Gwenda Stewart in the 'Dutch-clog' Austin Seven with which she broke Class H records; September 1931.
*(*The Autocar*)*

Chapter 9

1932: two miles a minute on 750cc

Nineteen-thirty-two opened with George Eyston awarded a BRDC Gold Star, mainly for his successful record onslaughts at Montlhéry. Although George had decided that if he wanted to exceed 100mph with the MG Midget he would have to use Pendine Sands and not the Paris track – in fact, he managed only 118.39mph on the sands – he was soon at Montlhéry with another car collecting another batch of records.

This time Eyston used a 4-litre straight-eight Delage sports chassis (the type wherein the OH valves were pushrod-operated with the valve springs mounted on the rocker arms, isolated from engine heat and exerting more leverage). The car was endowed with a very attractive but straightforward racing body, the eight exhaust outlets on the offside merging into a single straight exhaust pipe. Using BP fuel and Castrol oil, this Delage set out to capture world and Class C records.

It wasn't a very enjoyable ride, for the car had been planned for French drivers of small stature. Eyston found himself sitting well above the aero-screen, his face in the freezing blast of air, for a sharp east wind was blowing about the track. Moreover, Kaye Don rose from a sick bed against doctor's orders and flew from Croydon to Paris in order to help Eyston and Denly with the run. Eyston started before breakfast and secured the world 500-kilometre and three-hour records at 117.80mph and 117.83mph respectively, and the Class C 200-mile and 500-mile records at speeds of 117.47mph and 116.74mph before, frozen stiff, he pulled in for a much-needed meal.

Kaye Don took over, then later Denly and Eyston resumed. The sun came out but did nothing to relieve the bitter cold of the

February afternoon, although George must have been cheered to find that an aeroplane carrying a cinematograph operator had some difficulty keeping pace with the speeding Delage.

After three hours the Dunlop tyres on the back wheels were changed; after the car had been circulating for six hours the full set of wheels was replaced, and at nine hours a fresh offside back wheel was put on. After twelve hours darkness fell and the Delage, running beautifully, was brought in after having secured five additional records: the world 1000-kilometres at 117mph; the world six-hours at 117.12mph; the world 1000-mile and 2000-kilometre honours at 116.36 and 116.08mph respectively, and the Class C twelve-hour record at 112.03mph.

This book is largely a chronicle of record-breaking which, it should be appreciated, was achieved under winter conditions twenty-nine years ago by a virtually standard 4-litre car, and inclusive of pit-stops.

Eyston (who had, at this time, achieved some notoriety by owning a pet tiger) next cast his eye upon the world twelve- and twenty-four-hour records with his Panhard-Levassor. Looking at long distance 3-litre class records, we find that a Citroën had been busy again, cleaning up some of these: C and L Marchand, Forteu, Combette and L de Presale drove the car for an oil company and annexed the Class C 5000-mile record at 70.90mph, the three-day record at 70.82mph, the 10,000-kilometres at 114.04mph, and the four-day record at 70.79mph. Consistent motoring indeed, with all repairs being made from spares carried on the car. The Citroën, in fact, carried on successfully for 15,000 miles, or 11 days.

A most interesting aspect of record work arose in March. It had previously been assumed that short distance records, such as the flying-start kilometre and mile, could not be attempted on Montlhéry because they had to be made over a measured distance in both directions: in fact, the AIACR regulations stipulated this if such records were attempted on a *road*. But where a track was concerned they permitted these records to be taken over one complete lap of more than twice the stipulated distance, because, it was argued, in the course of a lap the car would have gone with and against any prevailing wind.

This premise, on a track sheltered by steep banking, is open to doubt and discussion but, the RAC having made known this AIACR ruling, meant that Montlhéry could obviously be used for these high-speed record attempts, rather than using some obscure, temporarily closed public road, or sands.

Albert Divo immediately availed himself of this new discovery, his Bugatti taking the flying-start kilometre and mile records in Class E in the course of an hour run. Incidentally, although similar tactics would have been permissible at Brooklands, there the track was closed and short distance records were taken in both directions, thus ensuring complete accuracy, which was important with split-second timing by automatically-actuated electrical timing apparatus.

Gwenda Stewart had not yet been active in 1932, because she had had to be taken quickly from Montlhéry to a nursing home in Fitzroy Square for an emergency operation, but the Citroën went on going round and round, seeking records over a prodigiously long distance and duration.

Meanwhile, that master of recordmen, G E T Eyston, was calmly preparing for his onslaught on that extremely difficult and highly coveted record, the world one-hour, with the by-no-means-young Panhard-Levassor. His first attempt ended in disaster, when he ran over what appeared to be a piece of rag or a dead bird on the track but was, in fact, a lump of broken concrete. This caused one of the special thin-tread Dunlop track tyres on a back wheel to burst with such a loud report that Ernest Eldridge thought the car had gone through the retaining wall.

Mention of the retaining wall reminds me that part of this was missing and that Eyston found driving along this section of the bankinq distinctly unpleasant. Beyond the top of the banking was just space!

The history of the world hour record up to the time of Eyston's attempt was as follows:

Eyston's Panhard-Levassor on the banking. (The Autocar)

Above: George E T Eyston at the wheel of the big sleeve-valve Panhard in 1932.

*Left: George Eyston's Panhard-Levassor breaks the world hour record in 1932. (*The Autocar*)*

*Below: George Eyston's straight-eight Delage in 1932. (*The Autocar*)*

1907 S F Edge (Napier) 70.07mph (Brooklands)
1907 W T Clifford Earp (Thames) 76.26mph (Brooklands)
1908 F Newton (Napier) 85.32mph (Brooklands)
1909 C M Smith (Thames) 89.51mph (Brooklands)
1912 D Resta (Sunbeam) 92.45mph (Brooklands)
1912 V Héméry (Lorraine-Dietrich) 97.49mph (Brooklands)
1913 P Lambert (Talbot) 103.84mph (Brooklands)
1913 J Goux (Peugeot) 106.22mph (Brooklands)
1913 J Chassagne (Sunbeam) 107.95mph (Brooklands)
1924 J G Parry Thomas (Leyland-Thomas) 109.09mph
       (Brooklands)
1925 J G Parry Thomas (Leyland-Thomas) 110.69mph
       (Brooklands)
1925 Ortmans (Panhard-Levassor) 116.41mph (Montlhéry)
1926 Ortmans (Panhard-tuevassor) 120.24mph (Montlhéry)
1926 E A D Eldridge (s/c Miller) 126.59mph (Montlhéry)
1927 C Marchand (Voisin) 128.35mph (Montlhéry)

The record was now at a speed at which the engine could not be spared by throttling back, and the tyres were subjected to severe stresses for the entire sixty minutes. Parry Thomas, indeed, had taken the record to 109.09mph, including a stop to have all wheels changed and the inevitable extra time loss resultant from coming in and accelerating away. So George Eyston had a tough task facing him, especially as the big 8-litre Panhard-Levassor was not a new car, was high-built and heavy on tyres, and needed great physical strength to pull it off the Montlhéry bankings. Moreover, as Eyston climbed into the narrow cockpit of this long, slim car, surrounded by a group of mechanics and other well-wishers, it was inclined to rain and weather conditions were poor, though perhaps Eyston welcomed rain on the track to cool the tyres.

Soon the Panhard-Levassor was speeding round, close to the edge of the banking, its Knight sleeve-valve engine held to around 2800rpm. On and on it went, without a sign of distress from car, man or tyres. The world hour record fell at 130.73mph, and, on the way, Eyston annexed the world 100-kilometre (131.80mph);

100-mile (131.67mph), and 200-kilometre (131.13mph) records. These also ranked as international Class B records, and in addition the big Panhard claimed the Class B 50-kilometre record at 130.79mph The best lap was covered at 137.83mph.

In the case of his Delage records Eyston had been able to advertise BP fuel, Castrol oil, KLG sparking plugs, Delco-Rémy ignition, Smiths carburetter, Ashby steering wheel, Moseley Float-on-Air cushions, Capasco brake linings, and Anti-fyre fire extinguishers. The splendid hour record with the Panhard-Levassor brought more publicity for BP, Castrol, KLG, Ashby, Capasco and Moseley.

The Panhard then came over to Brooklands for a highly dramatic BRDC British Empire Trophy Race on the outer circuit, which had a very odd result, the race, on appeal, being taken from Eyston who had averaged 126.35mph – but that's another story which I have set down elsewhere!*

Over at Montlhéry, the Citroën, now known as 'Rosalie', went on and on ... It finished finally, having covered 80,000 miles at 64mph; the only rumour of a reply to Citroën's challenge centred around an Invicta.

Then, in this eventful year, disaster overtook the Montlhéry track. Early one morning – about 1am – the nightwatchman saw an orange glow by the home banking and, upon investigation, found one of the under-banking sheds well alight. Trying to open the door of Mrs Stewart's shed in order to save her Derby-Miller, he broke the key in the lock. By this time the row of sheds was on fire, flames leaping higher than the retaining wall round the rim of the banking. Eventually Jean, the Hawkes-Stewart mechanic, arrived on the scene, broke open the shed door with a crowbar, went in where others refused to follow, fitted all four wheels to the Derby-Miller (which was up on jacks) and somehow pushed it off these and out of the shed with burning wood falling all around him. He dashed in again and saved the single-seater Morgan, after which the ceiling caved in and the shed went up in flames.

The team's entire equipment, all the Miller spares, their special tools and personal equipment, and the ex-Jappic HS cyclecar was

The History of Brooklands Motor Course.

lost. In other sheds the Bugatti with which Albert Divo had taken short distance records, four Citroëns, and many valuable engines and other material, were destroyed. Worse still, the concrete piers carrying the banking had cracked with the heat and damaged several sections of the track, which had to be closed for extensive repairs. Eyston's Panhard was not involved and duly made a *tour d'honneur* at Le Mans before the twenty-four-hour race.

Naturally enough, the fire held up all track activity at Montlhéry for a few weeks, but repairs were completed earlier than had at first been anticipated, and re-opening of the course coincided with the news that Studebaker would probably accept Citroën's challenge. Alas, legal difficulties relating to claims for losses caused a hold-up beyond that necessitated by the actual repairs.

The first record attempt after the track was declared open, but with a speed limit of 90mph (which enabled a lot of the customary testing to proceed) was, as one might have expected, by George Eyston. He wanted to try for the 1½-litre Class F twenty-four-hour record with one of the new 53 x 95.07mm six-cylinder Riley cars, with triple SU carburetters. The attempt was managed by Ernest Eldridge, and the co-drivers were Eyston's usual partner, Denly, and E Maclure, the well-known Riley driver.

The hazards were considerable, for repairs were not properly concluded, and a short distance after the timing line the track narrowed to less than a quarter of its usual width, there being a patch of unfinished concrete on the right, with a gaping hole covered in scaffolding beyond that. As if all this wasn't sufficient to deter most drivers, Eyston found he had to go higher up the banking than the narrow part of the track allowed for when the Riley was lapping at 95mph, so was forced to swerve down on to the smooth new concrete and then up again, with the prospect of falling through the gap had the car failed to respond. (I can hardly imagine the Brooklands authorities letting racing cars loose under such conditions!)

Anyway, at 3.30pm on 25 October, Eldridge waved Eyston away, who opened by lapping fast, anxious to gain time while daylight lasted. He continued to go round with great regularity for five hours, by which time it was dark and the outline of the track, including the 'precipice', was picked out with red road menders' lanterns. The Riley also had two headlamps set close together and two spotlamps on the nearside.

Its way thus illuminated, the Riley continued, driven now by Maclure. Later Albert Denly took over, to be greeted by fantastic conditions as a storm broke over Montlhéry. Rain lashed down in torrents, the spray flung up by the exposed front wheels causing the spotlamps' beams to dazzle the driver, who was wet to the skin as he sat huddled in the cockpit. The wind, increasing to gale force, blew the hurricane lamps out of place and caused one to upset, so that a trail of blazing paraffin ran down the track. But Denly stuck it out and the Class F twelve-hour record fell at 92.83mph, the Riley having covered 1113.8 miles. Just imagine the monotony, on a short course like Montlhéry!

As the car came in all four wheels were changed for those shod with the non-skid tyres used in practice. Soon the Class F 2000 kilometre record fell at 91.68mph, but disappointment followed when the Riley ran out of fuel and came to rest on the back stretch of the track. It was hastily replenished, but the scuttle tank had sprung a leak and fuel was flowing over the driver's legs. Eldridge drove rapidly to Montlhéry village and bought three clamps, with which a temporary repair was effected, aided by much soap. Fortunately this held, and although the ignition distributor and a plug had to be changed later, losing the Riley 17min 20sec, it had been running so well that it remained ahead of record schedule.

Then an oil pipe broke, but by that time the Class F twenty-four-hour record had been taken from André Boillot's Peugeot at 82.41mph (1977.8 miles), and the Riley had also taken the Class F 3000-kilometre record at 82.54mph. Incidentally, the 2000-kilometre record had stood since 1922, when the side-valve Aston Martin 'Bunny' had established it at Brooklands. Again, Eyston's usual accessories, together with the Rotax electrical equipment, André Telecontrol shock absorbers, Tecalemit oil cooler, and Laminex safety glass windscreen, came in for much praise. Thus was Montlhéry re-opened after damage by fire, several pressmen having come along to see the Riley embark on its long run.

By December record-breaking activity was back to normal. A sixteen-cylinder Maserati on Pirelli tyres was after Eyston's world hour record; Eyston had hopes of raising the twenty-four-hour record with the Delage, and 750cc class records were under attack. Unhappily, the Maserati, lapping at nearly 137mph and on its thirteenth lap, crashed after leaving the west banking, ending up behind the pits, its driver, Ruggeri, flung out and instantly killed. The cause was never clear, but the driver was inexperienced in driving at Montlhéry. The tyres were intact.

Undeterred, Eyston, wearing his asbestos overalls, brought out the supercharged MG Midget, with an engine taken from the burnt-out Ex 120, and exceeded 120mph for the first time in a 750cc car. Much earlier in the year Eyston had just failed to clock two-miles-a-minute at Pendine.

For these records the MG had a covered cockpit. It was brought out on 13 December. At first the time-keepers only clocked the little green projectile for two laps, and although the Class H kilometre and mile records had been broken, they had not been raised to over 120mph, so, typically, George went off again. However, rain began to fall and although he found the new stretch of concrete perfectly joined to the old, it was very smooth and therefore terribly slippery, grit not helping to any extent, meaning that Eyston had to lift his foot momentarily as he came off the new patch.

Smaller wheels were then fitted to lower the gear ratio, the oil changed, and plugs inspected. Eyston – who could hardly have forgotten his ordeal by fire on the previous MG attempt – again inserted his bulky athlete's body into the cockpit. The 'lid' was closed and away he went. This time there was no mistake. The revs climbed even higher than the 6300 figure achieved in the earlier attempt, Eyston didn't cut out the engine, and after eight laps he had done it: the kilometre at 120.56mph, the mile at exactly the same speed, five kilometres at 120.52mph, five miles at 116.71mph, and ten kilometres at 117.42mph. After that Ernest Eldridge took Eyston, Letorey (the track manager) and M Carpe (the time-keeper) out to lunch *avec* champagne!

Eyston used BP fuel, Castrol oil, Dunlop tyres, and his usual items, the steering wheel now a Dover and the instruments Jaeger. The supercharger was a Powerplus, sucking from an SU carburetter.

Soon afterwards a J3 MG Midget, driven by Eyston, Tommy Wisdom and Denly, captured Class H records for 1000-miles (69.19mph), 2000-kilometres (69.95mph), and twenty-four hours (1694.64 miles, 70.61mph). Because of the slippery section of the track the Delage record attack was postponed until 1933.

This twenty-four hour run had not been without incident, for the car broke a petrol pipe and had to be pushed to its depôt by Wisdom, where a further twenty minutes were lost whilst repairs were carried out. Then, when Denly was driving, ignition trouble cost the J3 MG another fifteen minutes. But Eyston, taking over, held steadfastly to the agreed 75mph lap speed, refusing to push the car too hard, and was duly rewarded. This run ended triumphantly at 3pm, and by 6am the following morning Eyston's men were sleepily trudging round Montlhéry placing red lanterns on the track. Eyston then got into the unlit cockpit of the single-seater 'Magic Midget', and half an hour later on this bleak morning of 21 December, 1932, having warmed up the car, set off, lapping fast at 95mph, then at 100mph. Record after record passed from Austin to MG: the Class H 200-kilometres at 95.52mph; the 200-mile at 95.02mph, and the three-hours at 94.59mph. After Denly took over, the 500-kilometre record fell at 91.7mph.

An oil leak caused slight alarm, but the little green MG went on and on, round and round, until, as darkness fell on the concrete bankings, the twelve-hour class record was taken at 86.67mph, and MG was able to claim the unique distinction of dominating Class H (up to 750cc) in the field of record-breaking.

A publicity stunt arranged by the owners of Montlhéry in March 1932. Marcel Doret's Dewoitine aeroplane races a Bugatti T51 driven by Divo. The aircraft won at a speed of 209.670km/h, while the Bugatti achieved 206.321km/h.

Un match original : auto contre avion

Un match vient d'avoir lieu sur et au-dessus de la piste de vitesse de l'autodrome de Monthéry. L'aviateur Doret, sur avion Dewoitine, et l'automobiliste Divo, sur sa voiture Bugatti de course, tous deux as de la vitesse, ont disputé une course sur quatre tours de piste. L'aviateur battit l'automobiliste avec 209 km 670 à l'heure contre 206 km 321.

Chapter 10

1933: the Maserati–Alfa-Romeo duel

1933 opened with a letter from Gwenda Stewart featuring in a well-known British weekly motor paper, correcting the impression that a section of the Montlhéry banking above the point of the previous year's disastrous fire was dangerously slippery for fast cars. Gwenda pointed out that the mistake of using the wrong material when the track was re-surfaced at this part was quickly discovered, so that difficulty was encountered only on the bottom third of the banking, used only by normal cars for low-speed tests. Fast cars going higher up the Montlhéry banking were unaffected. Mrs Stewart, writing from St Cloud, emphasized her point by remarking that she had no aspirations whatsoever for the death of a heroine, yet had been able to lap at 134mph in the wet on her first visit to the track after the fire the previous May, and in a car that 'normally takes a comparatively low line on the banking'; presumably her Derby-Miller.

She went on to remark that the track was in excellent condition, joining of the old and new parts having been perfectly accomplished. She said she wrote 'in a pure sense of fair play due to that much-afflicted and unlucky organization, the *Societé de l'Autodrome de Montlhéry.*'

Mrs Stewart had her eye on Eldridge's 2-litre flying mile record of 136.26mph, and had obtained permission to be timed over a complete lap in attempting the flying-start kilometre and mile records. She had fully recovered from her recent illness, and the Derby-Miller likewise from the effects of the fire. A new engine was installed by Douglas Hawkes, and on her second run Gwenda lapped at 140mph.

The next piece of activity centred round Kaye Don and George

Eyston, who raised the international Class C record to 123.01mph, and the 200-kilometre record to 122.36mph with the 4.9-litre Bugatti, Don handing over to Eyston a few laps from the end of the run, by which time the back axle was in a pretty poor state. Citroën was also at it again, a 1½-litre car circulating on one of those interminable endurance runs, the first records to fall being the Class F 4000-miles at 67.1mph, and the three-days at 61.8mph.

This Citroën was the famous 'Petite Rosalie' and it was accompanied by 'Agatha', a sister car. The former car had gone on to take the 5000-mile and four-day Class records before stopping with a broken ball-bearing, the luckless driver having to effect repairs with spares and tools carried on the car, while 'Agatha' continued on its way. In Class C a Ford held records from 5000 miles to 20,000-kilometres, and from three to seven days at speeds of just above 78mph, the car sponsored by Yacco oil.

In due course Gwenda Stewart secured the 2-litre mile record at 137.85mph: her car now called a Derby Special because most of the original Miller parts had been eliminated.

H Widengren then took out a very special Amilcar Six with a plain bearing engine – the beautiful little 1100cc twin overhead-camshaft supercharged unit set *désaxé* in the frame. It had a fully streamlined single-seater body. Widengren took the international Class G fifty-kilometre, fifty-mile, 100-mile and 200-kilometre records, and also the coveted 'hour' at 115.31mph. These records were formerly held by F W Dixon's Riley, which had averaged 110.93mph for the hour on Brooklands. Gwenda Stewart then decided to lift her mile record higher still, and after a very exciting run in the 1.6-litre front-wheel-drive Derby (which broke a shock absorber and had a gusty wind to contend with), managed a splendid 139.13mph. It was a case of coming crabwise off the steep bankings, and Mrs Stewart missed the kilometre record by as little as .006 of a second. At the other extreme Trebuh challenged the 3-litre class standing-start kilometre record with a 2 .3 Bugatti and raised it to 80.83mph.

111

Meanwhile, the Yacco-sponsored single-seater Citroën Ten (the four-cylinder 1452cc model), was piling up mileage at the rate of 1400 miles a day, covering a fantastic 68,000 miles in under two months. Innumerable Class F records fell, the car lapping relentlessly day and night. Earlier records were taken at 57-58mph, but as engine and chassis bearings loosened, up climbed the speed. This rather overshadowed the more private venture of the Hon Mrs Victor Bruce and her husband, who drove a 7hp Jowett saloon towing a 100-gallon petrol trailer to Montlhéry, covered 2772 miles non-stop in seventy-two hours, refuelling from the trailer, and then drove the outfit back to England, to be welcomed in Bradford by the Lord Mayor and Deputy Mayoress. They had averaged a very consistent 38.54mph on the track.

Such endurance stuff was completely overshadowed for a while by the remarkable Stewart-Hawkes-Cann *équipe*, for the Derby – a car of only 1660cc – set the 2-litre class mile and kilometre records to 143.29mph, a higher speed than the Brooklands lap record or, in fact, any record set on any European track. Not content with that, Gwenda Stewart was soon out again, accomplishing a lap time of 145.94mph, a new Montlhéry record.

Because part of the banked circuit was required for the French Grand Prix, the Citroën record run had to stop temporarily, after it had taken or established 128 international Class F records and 43 world records, 120,000 miles covered in 2076hr 13min 14sec. While the Grand Prix was held the Derby occupied a place of honour in the paddock, Gwenda Stewart keen to use it to set the hour record to around 137mph. Before the track was closed Sénéchal tested a curious twin crankshaft, supercharged, all-independently-sprung two-stroke single-seater which got up to 120mph.

The 1933 French Grand Prix was run over 500 kilometres of the combined road and track circuit, which measured 12.5 kilometres. This race had originally attracted twenty-eight entries, but the new Bugattis were not ready, and Sir Henry Birkin was suffering from blood poisoning, from which he subsequently died. Starters dwindled to nineteen.

As the field roared off, negotiating Bruyères hairpin, Les Biscornes, Forêt corner, Gendarme corner and the Faye hairpin, to appear round the steep banking at the end of the opening lap, Tazio Nuvolari, in his red straight-eight Alfa-Romeo led from Campari's Maserati and Taruffi's Alfa-Romeo. Chiron, followed by all French eyes, held fourth place in another Alfa-Romeo. Already Earl Howe was at the pits calling for fresh plugs for his 2.3 Bugatti – it was not Molsheim's day.

Nuvolari set a fast pace and, trying to keep up with him, Campari equalled Montlhéry's road circuit lap record of 85.5mph. Lehoux had a rod emerge from the crankcase of his Alfa-Romeo. Nuvolari had held his advantage for six laps and Chiron, driving his Alfa-Romeo from the top of the banking, had come up to third place when both drivers came into the pits together.

They soon succumbed to back-axle failures. This put the burly Campari, noted opera singer as well as talented racing driver, in the lead, chased by Etancelin. Czaykowski consumed rear tyres on the big hour record Bugatti and finally retired with a broken ball-race in the gearbox.

This all happened in the days when pit-stops were an exciting aspect of long distance races, and after thirteen laps Campari pulled in to have his back tyres changed. He was away in fifty-two seconds, but this was too long: Taruffi and Etancelin had gone by. Etancelin soon took the lead from Taruffi, and these two were followed by Zehender's monoposto Maserati and the Alfa-Romeos of Moll and Sommer. George Eyston found his Alfa-Romeo too high-geared for the hilly section of Montlhéry's circuit, and had to be content with seventh place.

In trying to increase his lead Etancelin set a new lap record of 86.2mph, but not to be outdone, Campari began to clip fifteen seconds a lap off the lead Etancelin that held, lapping at 86.56mph in his two-seater Maserati. Campari's lead was assured when Etancelin stopped in his turn for fresh tyres, fuel and oil, the stop costing him 115 seconds.

At twenty laps, or half-distance, Campari led from Taruffi, who was assisted at his pit-stop by Nuvolari. The latter, after wheels had been changed and the car re-fuelled, vaulted into the driving seat. Alas, after only two laps he had broken this car as well ...

At the end of thirty laps Campari came in for another change of tyres, all four wheels being attended to in a mere 43.6 seconds, whereupon Etancelin resumed the lead by thirty-six seconds. Four laps later Campari had closed to within 112 seconds of his rival Etancelin, a wool merchant from Rouen, troubled now by clutch seizure. One more lap and the blue Alfa-Romeo led the Maserati by a bare 2.2 seconds, and then, on lap thirty-fve, the gap closed to just 1.2 seconds.

The French Grand Prix of 1933 now took a dramatic turn. The two opposing makes came round the banking virtually side-by-side with only two laps to go. Everyone expected Campari to snatch the lead but instead he cut out his engine and rolled to his pit. The burly Italian had felt rain and, for his final effort, wanted non-skid back tyres. The change was effected in fifty-six seconds and the Maserati, no. 32, accelerated away with only fifteen miles in which to catch the Alfa-Romeo. It seemed that Campari had thrown away the race, for as the pair entered the last lap he was 23.2 seconds in arrears, and at the finishing line the officials had Etancelin's number ready beside the chequered flag, confident that the Alfa-Romeo must win. But no, the clutch refused to free, and Etancelin bent the sturdy gear lever in his fruitless efforts to change gear. The Maserati drew ahead and won by fifty-two seconds, Etancelin finishing unhappily in second place.

The winner had been driving for 3hr 48min 45.5sec, to average 81.48mph. George Eyston, by steady driving, was third, his Alfa-Romeo a lap behind the leaders. Sommer finished fourth, his Alfa-Romeo on the same lap as Eyston; Guy Moll's Alfa-Romeo was fifth, two laps in arrears, and the only other car to be placed was the Alfa-Romeo driven by Villars, which was running six laps behind the leaders.

During the race an amusing battle of another kind had been fought, when lawless spectators who had scaled the banking not in use were apprehended by the police and sent sliding downwards to safety.

After being the venue of this classic Grand Prix the Paris Autodrome resumed its usual role of hosting the Derby, Campari's Maserati, and a streamlined 2-litre Hotchkiss intent on challenging records. A curious little 495cc Standard two-stroke, driven by Fachsenfeld and Meyer, took Class 1 fifty-kilometre, fifty-mile, 100-mile, 500-kilometre, and six-hour records, the fastest being the fifty-mile at 80.27mph; the tiny car managed to maintain 67.7mph for the six hours.

The endurance record Citroën was also on its way again with the 129 day record in the bag, at 58.19mph. This Citroën finally called it a day after 300,000 kilometres, in which distance it took or established 296 records, averaging just over 58mph overall for 133 days. Montlhéry seemed quite a lonely place after it left!

Not surprisingly, the next bout of activity concerned George Eyston. This inveterate record breaker came out with a businesslike straight-eight Delage, intent on the world twenty-four-hour record, but the battery shorted, the car caught fire, and some damage was done to the track, which delayed attempts by the Derby and a big Panhard-Levassor. However, before this the Delage had broken the 200-mile Class record at 117.57mph. Then, when the carefully prepared Derby Special was let loose, Mrs Stewart increased her own Class ten-mile record to a splendid 138.34mph.

As Motor Show time approached all manner of cars gathered at Montlhéry to challenge records in many different classes. John Cobb's big new Napier Lion-engined car, after tyre tests at Brooklands, was ready for a go at the world twenty-four-hour record, drivers and crew flying by airliner to Paris. Alas, it was late in the year for a run of this duration, twelve hours of darkness and considerable mist the prospect to be faced. The arrangement of one type of tyre on the front wheels and another type on the back wheels could only be proved satisfactory or otherwise after 200 miles had been covered, and the heavy wheels cost at least a minute at each pit-stop. Finally, the attempt was postponed whilst

John Cobb in the Napier-Railton, 1933. The Brooklands silencers were not needed at Montlhéry.
(The Autocar)

these difficulties were resolved. An Austin Seven attempt, too, fell through due to various mechanical troubles, but Vasselle had the very beautiful streamlined track Hotchkiss going well on test. The Derby Special came out for its long-awaited onslaught on the hour record, but a blower-drive tooth failed on the line.

Cobb was awaiting news of speeds put up in America by a Pierce-Arrow to see whether or not his world records up to six hours in the Napier-Railton would stand. In the end he was credited with the world 200-mile record at 126.44mph, 500-kilometres at 123.63mph, 500-miles at 123.27mph, 1000-kilometres at 122.05mph, the three-hours at 124.33mph, the six-hours at 122.62mph, and some Class A records as well, including the hour at 126.83mph. The Pierce-Arrow had possibly gone faster but the AIACR had not been told about it.

Murray Jamieson had taken out the new Rootes supercharged Austin single-seater, and was rewarded with the Class H five-mile record at 119.38mph, the ten-kilometres at 119.39mph, and the ten-miles at 119.18mph, thus relieving Eyston and the MG Midget of these honours and going almost as quickly as that car, Eyston's best being 120.56mph. MG soon reversed that situation, Albert Denly taking the Magic Midget out at Montlhéry and lapping at 128.62mph, the little single-seater reaching 130 at times. In warm weather which helped to carburate the alcohol fuel, and managed by Eyston, the attempt was extremely successful. The Class mile and kilometre record fell at 128.62mph, the five-miles at 127.80mph, the ten-kilometres at 127.23mph, and the ten-mile record at 125.43mph. The little engine, which was the one from Hamilton's TT car, reached 6600rpm on one or two occasions. Discs were used on the front wheels, and, as a light breeze got up, Denly had some anxious moments correcting the MG's desire to wander.

The Hotchkiss, too, was now doing its stuff, Eyston, Vasselle and Denly taking the Class E 500-mile record at 101.13mph, the 1000-kilometres at 101.55mph, and the six-hours at 101.50mph.

Citroën, to set the seal on its magnificent long distance records, challenged anyone to beat 'Rosalie' by putting up a 7 million franc stake, the challenger to embody no modification beyond those which Citroën had allowed.

As 1933 drew to a close, Veyron took out a 1½-litre Bugatti and captured various Class F records, including the hour at 119.01mph, having previously set the 200-mile record at 115.49mph. This achievement was somewhat overshadowed when Denly drove the MG Midget for an hour, to average 110.87mph from a standing start, taking the fifty-kilometre Class record at 115mph, the fifty-mile record at 114.47mph, and the 100-mile record at 111.1 7mph on its way. Eyston also had the Panhard out, looking towards the world hour record, and broke Czaykowski's Bugatti 100-kilometre record with a speed of 134.73mph, taking also the Class B fifty-kilometre and fifty-mile records at 133.64 and 134.16mph respectively.

Zehender now appeared with a 3-litre Maserati and, in spite of the car suffering from fuel starvation to its eight cylinders, took four Class records from Divo's Bugatti up to 100 miles at 132.43mph before giving up. While waiting for better weather for his hour record attempt with the big Panhard-Levassor, Eyston, aided by Maclure, broke three of Veyron's 1½-litre records with a Riley, including 500-miles at 110.55mph, the car exceeding 112mph for three hours.

Snow and ice then descended on Montlhéry, but not before Arthur Duray and J and H Gavardte had broken Riley Class G records up to twenty-four hours with an Amilcar Six, averaging 85.07mph. Gwenda Stewart was invited, with Divo whom she had vanquished, to a pleasant little function given by the AC of the Ile de France, where she received a cup in recognition of having broken the Montlhéry lap record. Only the wintry weather was delaying her attempt on the 'hour'.

Etonian John Cobb, who took his Napier-Railton to Montlhéry and broke many long distance records in it.

La Petite Rosalie — the Yacco Citroën in 1933 with (opposite) one of its record certificates. (S A André Citroën)

Murray Jamieson in the Austin Seven that beat Eyston's MG records; 1933. (The Autocar)

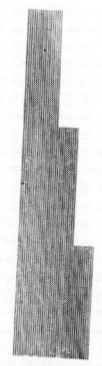

ASSOCIATION INTERNATIONALE DES AUTOMOBILE-CLUBS RECONNUS

CERTIFICAT DE RECORD

Les soussignés certifient au nom de
l'Association Internationale des Automobile-Clubs Reconnus que
le record du Monde des 300.000 kilomètres
a été établi du 15 Mars au 27 Juillet 1933
sur la piste de l'autodrome de Montlhéry
Distance parcourue 300.000 kilomètres
Temps 3209ᵍ 37 38ᵐ ⁴/₁₀₀   Vitesse moyenne 93.469 K.P.H. / 58.08 M.P.H.
Voiture **CITROEN** 1463ᶜᶜ
Engagée par la Société des **HUILES YACCO**
Pilotée par César Marchand, L. Marchand, Leroy de Presale,
Fortin, Bodecot, Vaillant, Combette et Bertaux

Délivré à Paris le 8 Septembre 1933

Le Secrétaire Général
de l'A.I.A.C.R.

Le Président de la Commission
Sportive Internationale

Gwenda Stewart in the famous Derby-Miller. Hawkes in cap and mechanic Fred Cann with beret.

*145.94mph, 28 May, 1933: the Derby Special sets
a lap record for the banked track. Pictured are:
Mrs Stewart (in crash helmet); Mr Douglas Hawkes
(bare-headed in suit, leaning over engine), and
Mr Fred Cann in overalls on his left. Note the
propellor used to drive an auxiliary oil scavenge
pump. (Wide World photos/Mr Fred Cann)*

George Eyston with the AEC diesel car which had a Chrysler chassis. (The Autocar)

Chapter 11

1934: the Napier-Railton goes over the wall

The weather in the Paris area in the New Year of 1934 was distinctly disagreeable, delaying several attempts on the world hour record by Zehender's Maserati, Eyston's big Panhard, and Gwenda Stewart's Derby, as was a Hotchkiss attempt on the forty-eight-hour record. For the same reason, John Cobb had not left for Montlhéry with the Napier-Railton.

The gap in the retaining fence remained a hazard, though it was now marked by a continuous black line painted on the banking a few feet from the top. Further consternation was caused by some Pierce-Arrow records, including the twenty-four hours, set up at Muroc in Utah, which the AIACR had neither confirmed nor disallowed.

Eventually Veyron led the way, taking six Class F 1½-litre records with a straight-eight Bugatti, at speeds of 116.51mph for 200-miles, 114.29mph for 500-miles, and 112.98mph for the full six-hours.

Next it was George Eyston's turn. Eyston had a very difficult task to accomplish. His world hour record with the 8-litre Panhard-Levassor had been broken by Count Czaykowski, who had averaged 132.87mph at the Avus track outside Berlin in spite of having to slow for the corners which connected the straights. Eyston had the streamlining of the venerable Panhard single-seater improved and went out at Montlhéry to try to regain his lost laurels.

The Panhard ran faultlessly, the Dunlop tyres survived, and Eyston cleverly raised the record by a just-sufficient margin at a speed of 133.01mph. On the day following this magnificent run, Eyston placed a wreath in memory of Czaykowski, who, since setting his record at Avus, had been killed at Monza. Records had for some time been successfully challenged at places other than Montlhéry and Brooklands. A reminder of this was provided when, at long last, the AIACR recognized a host of world and Class B records set up by Jenkins and a 7½-litre, twelve-cylinder Pierce-Arrow at Utah in 1933. These included the twelve- and twenty-four hours, at 120.58 and 117.82mph respectively. Then, on the difficult Avus track, Hans von Stuck broke the world hour record with what was virtually a road-racing Auto-Union, at 134.90mph. Thus did the task of establishing new records on Montlhéry's banked track become ever more difficult.

Undaunted, George Eyston, aided by Denly, took out the 2-litre Hotchkiss, this time running the very nicely streamlined car without the enclosed cockpit. They set Class E records for 1000-miles at 99.07mph, twelve-hours at 98.29mph, 2000-kilometres at 98.33mph, twenty-four-hours at 97.7mph, 3000-kilometres at 96.69mph, 4000-kilometres at 96.88mph, 5000-kilometres at 96.67mph, 4000-miles at 95.76mph, forty-eight hours at 95.36mph, and 1000-miles at 94.73mph, the last three being world records in addition – a very good run!

Eyston then went on to demonstrate the AEC diesel-engined saloon at Montlhéry. He had earlier shown it off at Brooklands in pouring rain, George enjoying the joke as he was in the dry; the spectators, as I well remember, huddled under umbrellas. In those days separate diesel records were not recognized, but the AEC did a lap at 115.41mph and was timed for ten kilometres at 115.07mph.

Citroën, having been successful at fantastically long duration records, failed on a forty-eight-hour attempt, but Eyston and Maclure had no trouble when they brought out the non-supercharged six-cylinder Riley, talking the Class F 1000 mile record up to 102.35mph, the twelve-hour record to 101.10mph, and the 2000-kilometre record to 101.04mph.

Then John Cobb's big car finally left for Montlhéry, Dunlop having supplied special outsize track tyres for the back wheels.

Cobb, Cyril Paul, Freddie Dixon and Charles Brackenbury went over in style in an Imperial Airways airliner, intent on lifting the world twenty-four-hour record to comfortably better than 120mph.

The big Napier-Railton duly started, timed by French timekeepers, with King Farlow doing his own timing for the beneft of Cobb's *équipe*. An elaborate signalling device, consisting of a semaphore arm illuminated after dark by little red bulbs, kept the drivers informed of whether to increase or decrease speed. The Napier-Railton rushed round and round in deceptive silence. Every 240 miles the car came to a standstill at its depôt and all four of the big wheels were changed, more National Benzole was added to the fuel tank, and Castrol oil and water in the appropriate places if needed.

The second attempt began just on midday one Monday in April, and by midnight the world twelve-hour record was in the possession of this determined team, at 121.19mph. Some speed had been held in reserve for making up time if conditions after dark had been unfavourable, but the Napier-Railton just went on and on faultlessly, although its creator, Reid A Railton, naturally watched anxiously, as did Norman Freeman of Dunlop, especially when a tyre tread was flumg off.

The driving seat was less comfortable than it should have been, and after a short spell Cyril Paul gave up, as his appendix was troubling him. It wasn't at all easy to maintain a lap speed of 120mph during the night, particularly as it began to rain at dawn. Yet the drivers coped admirably and it seemed that this special record-breaking giant, with its Napier Lion engine idling comfortably at two miles a minute, would achieve its objective.

Alas, it was not to be. Four hours from the end, while tough little Dixon was driving, a skid started as the Napier-Railton left the west banking, and although Dixon fought this all the way to the east banking, he was quite unable to retrieve the situation. The car slid, struck the retaining wall, put two wheels over the edge, and then ran down the banking and on to the infield. Only

Dixon's pride was hurt, but the Napier-Railton was extensively damaged and a Renault armoured caterpillar was needed to drag it out of the ditch. The chassis frame was dented, the sub-frame twisted, the wheels ruined, and slight damage sustained by the underparts of the engine and spring shackles.

However, world records for 1000-miles (122.82mph), six-hours (123.01mph), twelve-hours (121.19mph), 3000-kilometres (120.71mph), and 2000-miles (120.71mph) had been broken. These also, naturally, counted in Class A, and in addition the Napier-Railton secured the Class A 1000 mile record at 121.51mph and the 2000-kilometres record at 121.54mph.

The car carried its own, very excellent, headlamps but red lanterns were also placed round the track. The pit-stops came every 75 to 110 minutes, and occupied from fifty-two to fifty-eight seconds. This time included changing all four of the immense wheels, filling up, cleaning the windscreen, changing drivers, and running the car back a considerable distance in order to re-start the engine by pushing. One tyre apparently deflated slowly as the crashed car lay in the ditch, but it was claimed that a broken bottle caused the puncture. All tyres had been seen to be intact as the car plunged off the banking, so the unfortunate Dixon, who may have dozed, couldn't claim a tyre blow-out as an excuse for his spectacular accident!

Next, Mrs Stewart brought out the 1.6-litre Derby and pushed up three of her own records: the five-kilometres to 140.351mph; the five-miles to 140.16mph, and the ten-kilometres to 140.07mph.

For a spell Montlhéry became the haunt of bicycles fitted with airscrews, which refused to fly.

On the serious side Mrs Stewart was after the hour record, although her famous Derby was of only 1660cc. A streamlined Delahaye saloon sought the forty-eight-hour record, as did an ancient sleeve-valve Peugeot. The Delahaye duly triumphed, taking the world forty-eight-hour record at 109.52mph, and nine Class C records as well; also world honours for 4000-miles (110.39mph) and 5000-miles (110.26mph).

Eyston, joined by Dudley Froy, then set about cleaning up some of the Pierce-Arrow records established far away in Utah. Using the red Panhard-Levassor shod with Dunlop tyres, the pair increased the world Class A 200-mile record to 128.07mph, the three-hours to 126.22mph, the six-hours to 124.82mph, and the 500-miles to 126.45mph. Eyston then turned his attention to the diesel-engined AEC again, getting it over the flying kilometre at 120.22mph.

Montlhéry now busied itself with preparations for the French Grand Prix. I can well remember the intense excitement I felt at being able to see the fabulous Mercédès-Benz and Auto-Union teams in action at Donington Park, but that was not until 1937, whereas the French were able to see these extremely powerful German cars in action, close to Paris, in the first year of the 750kg formula. Indeed, a very intriguing field lined up at Montlhéry for the French Grand Prix, and tremendous crowds streamed out to the track to witness the forthcoming truly international battle.

A brave array of genuine Grand Prix cars took their places on the starting grid after parading before the grandstands. The spotless, red Alfa-Romeos were the Scuderia Ferrari twin-propeller-shaft 3.2-litre cars. The Auto-Unions had swastikas on their tails alongside the German colours. The 3.3-litre Bugattis carried the names of their drivers in silver lettering on their scuttles.

The Alfa-Romeos had arrived at Montlhéry first and had weighed out at 720.5, 726.5 and 730kg respectively. The Mercédès-Benz had tipped the scales at 737, 739 and 739.5kg; the Auto-Unions weighed 736.5, 7:38 and 740kg, and the Bugattis were 747, 747 and 749.5kg. The works Maserati was found to weigh 735kg, and Etancelin's Maserati 748.5kg.

At last they were on the starting grid. Montlhéry was a swarming mass of expectant humanity anxious for the silent pack to be unleashed. Stuck's Auto-Union and Varzi's Alfa-Romeo occupied the front row, with Caracciola's Mercédès-Benz and Momberger's Auto-Union behind. Next was the popular Louis Chiron in his Alfa-Romeo beside Nuvolari's Bugatti, and the Bugatti of Benoist.

Behind them were Dreyfus' Bugatti and Count Trossi's Alfa-Romeo, then von Brauchitsch's Mercédès-Benz, Zehender's red Maserati, and Etancelin's Maserati painted in the blue of France. Right at the back sat Fagioli in the third Mercédès-Benz. In practice the silver Mercédès had been terrifically fast but heavy on tyres; the Auto-Unions seemed to lack reliability; the Maseratis were difficult to handle; the Bugattis not really ready. Only the Scuderia Ferrari Alfa-Romeos were entirely at ease.

At the one minute signal the hitherto silent cars were started; a great pandemonium of sound and smoke smote the onlookers, and the blue starting flag went up. It wavered, upon which Chiron shot from third to first row. As the flag swept down, Chiron was away in the lead after a truly professional start.

Chiron completed his opening lap in 5min 29sec, coming off the east banking with Caracciola; Fagioli and Stuck behind him. On the next lap Stuck and Fagioli had passed Caracciola, but still the French driver in the Italian car led. Nuvolari's '3.3' Bugatti had stopped for a change of plugs.

Now von Stuck's rear-engined Auto-Union took the lead, and Fagioli's Mercédès-Benz was pressing Louis Chiron's Alfa-Romeo very hard – the Germans were piling on the pressure.

The pace was hot and Nuvolari, fed up with his Bugatti which refused to stay in gear, had handed over the car to Pierre Wimille, while Etancelin's Maserati was throwing oil about the cockpit, the driver climbing out to hold a voluble discussion with the mechanics.

On lap nine Brauchitsch came in and, although his Mercédès-Benz continued, it was obviously no longer a factor in the race, its exhaust crackle now very subdued. Then, on the tenth lap of this 311 mile race, Chiron took the lead again, for Stuck's Auto-Union was in trouble. Mercédès-Benz sensed this and Fagioli and Caracciola were speeded up, Fagioli breaking the lap record at 5min 8.3sec, equal to a lap speed of 90.67mph.

Stuck limped in, got out and took a long drink as the German mechanics refuelled his car and changed both back wheels, costing the Austrian 2min 35sec. Meanwhile, the two Mercédès-Benz were close on the tail of Chiron's Alfa-Romeo. Now both Momberger's Auto-Union and Brauchitsch's Mercédès-Benz retired; one with steering trouble and the other with a sick engine. Etancelin, too, threw in the towel.

The eyes of thousands of elated Frenchmen were watching Chiron, his Alfa-Romeo booming defiance at the snarling Mercédès-Benz. He was driving ever faster and faster to retain his lead, the race average climbing first to 87.77mph, then to 88.39mph. Fagioli set the lap record for the sinuous road circuit to 5min 6.3sec, to which Louis Chiron replied with 5min 6.0sec or 91.35mph.

This was racing at its fiercest and finest, and Mercédès-Benz had to give way to the meticulously prepared Ferrari Alfa-Romeos.

Just as Neubauer was preparing his mechanics for a routine pit-stop, Fagioli failed to appear. He had stopped out on the course. Moreover, to the consternation of the Stuttgart team, Caracciola's car was slowing, enabling Varzi's Alfa-Romeo to go through to second place. At the pits they refuelled the sole remaining Mercédès-Benz, gave it water and fresh back tyres in 1min 20sec, but to no avail: soon this car, too, came to rest and retired.

The French Grand Prix was now comfortably within the grasp of Alfa-Romeo. Chiron eased up; Varzi held second place, and Stuck's Auto-Union – its early fire subdued – ran badly in third place. Trossi had stopped to have the transmission of his Alfa-Romeo inspected, handing over to Guy Moll, but as Zehender's Maserati was running badly and the Bugatti challenge had never materialized, the Scuderia Ferrari had little to trouble them. Dreyfus' Bugatti refused to fire on the side starting handle and was retired with engine failure; Wimille still had plug and gearbox troubles to contend with. Only Benoist's Bugatti was running properly, albeit too slowly.

This was the age of enthralling pit-work, and although the race, as such, now lacked excitement, the spectators were able to see Chiron's leading Alfa-Romeo have all four wheels changed and fuel and water topped up in a time of 1min 39sec. Varzi led while this feverish yet apparently effortless work was going on, then he, in turn, came in, the Ferrari mechanics getting the same jobs completed in a mere 1min 30sec. Not to be outdone, Stuck's mechanics refuelled the Auto-Union in 1min 3sec whilst – to the crowd's delight – the tall Austrian had a gargle! Later this team got the time down to 1min 40sec, including changing the car's back wheels.

The Alfa-Romeos now dominated the race, both Chiron and Varzi coming in again later for fuel and tyres. Varzi had time to go for a short stroll, smoking a cigarette, Moll thus temporarily taking second place. Stuck's Auto-Union finally succumbed to a bad water leak. Even Benoist's Bugatti began to misfire, and the other Bugattis had been having a fearful time in the pits. Zehender's Maserati had the back axle come adrift on one side.

So, under a broiling sun, Chiron came home a popular winner, three minutes or so ahead of Varzi. Moll went to his pit, was promptly shooed out again, and ran on to complete the Alfa-Romeo grand slam. The result was:

1st   L Chiron (Alfa-Romeo) 85.05mph
2nd   A Varzi (Alfa-Romeo) 83 80mph
3rd   Count Trossi/G Moll (Alfa-Romeo) 83.447mph
Flagged off: R Benoist (Bugatti) 36 laps
Retired: Zehender (Maserati), broken spring clips, 33 laps; Stuck (Auto-Union), engine trouble, 32 laps; Nuvolari/Wimille (Bugatti), engine trouble, 17 laps; Dreyfus (Bugatti), engine failure, 16 laps; Caracciola (Mercédès-Benz), engine trouble, 15 laps; Fagioli (Mercédès-Benz), brake trouble, 14 laps; Brauchitsch (Mercédès-Benz), engine trouble, 11 laps; Etancelin (Maserati), engine trouble, 11 laps; Momberger (Auto-Union), steering maladies, 10 laps.

Mrs Stewart's Derby Special after its crash in 1934.
*(*The Autocar*)*

The 1934 500 kilometre French Grand Prix had certainly taken its toll! After this, Montlhéry reverted to its status of test track and record-breaking venue, untroubled by litter and seething crowds. Gwenda Stewart got out her famous front-drive Derby Special and raised the lap record to a fantastic and courageous 147.79mph. However, she was combining demonstration with scientific research, cutting the engine at full bore after the timed lap so that Douglas Hawkes and their English mechanic, Fred Cann, could observe the condition of the experimental Bosch plugs. This caused the Derby to snake as Gwenda thrust it out of gear and turned off the fuel. It shot down the banking into the infield, up the banking again, teetered on two wheels, fell back on to all four, then came down and rammed the bank, both front wheels torn off: a sad end to a very fine run. Mrs Stewart was cut near one eye, concussed slightly and suffering from torn and bruised muscles, but the flying start kilometre and mile Class records had been secured, as well as the Montlhéry lap record. Luckily damage to the car was less than it might have seemed, whllst the most serious outward sign of Gwenda's injuries was a fine black eye.

Eyston, this time partnered by Handley, had a crack at the forty-eight-hour record with the Hotchkiss, and even wanted to try for the world hour record with his single-seater supercharged MG Magnette 'The Humbug' — so called on account of its striped paint — notwithstanding the fact that the 1100cc car would be up against the Auto-Union's time of 134.90mph.

Eyston actually began by wiping out the Amilcar's short distance Class G records, the MG clocking 128.70mph for the kilometre and mile, the five-kilometres at 128.69mph, and the five-miles at 128.53mph. The Magnette went on to collect the fifty-kilometre Class record at 119.84mph; the fifty-miles at 120.72mph; the 100-kilometres at 121.65mph; the 100-miles at 121.13mph, and the 200-kilometres at 120.82mph. It kept going for one hour at over two miles a minute: 120.88mph.

Then, at the year's end, Maillard-Brune and Druck took the

Class H (750cc) twenty-four-hour record at 76.30mph and the Class 2000-kilometre record at 76.18mph with an MG Midget. Now repaired, the Derby had been lapping unofficially at 148mph.

As 1934 gave way to 1935, so many records were falling at Utah, Avus and on temporarily-closed Italian roads, that it was becoming more and more difficult to set new ones at Montlhéry.

Chapter 12

1935: the revenge of Mercédès-Benz

Gwenda Stewart, who *was* Montlhéry, hurt herself in a ski-ing accident during the winter of 1934-5, but obviously intended to continue motor racing, and had arranged things so that she was no longer committed to driving only cars of Derby manufacture. The French Grand Prix was again to be run over the road circuit, and although the date fixed was 23 June, Auto-Union sent a deputation to look at the course late in March.

Montlhéry was comparatively inactive during 1935, but around April Fool's Day the Class F 2000-mile record was broken at 96.5mph by a straight-eight Bugatti driven by Veyron, Labric and Villeneuve, the car going on to secure the 3000-kilometre record at 92.68mph, and the twenty-four-hours at 91.94mph.

Maillard-Brune went well in a 750cc MG belonging to Menier, the chocolate king, beating several '1100s' in a small race.

Montlhéry then became animated with preparations for the French Grand Prix. (Incidentally, there is nothing very new in travelling by air to foreign motor races from this country. In 1935 you could fly from Heston, where the Vintage Sports Car Club has held driving test meetings in recent years, leaving at 9am and returning from a point near Montlhéry at 7pm the same day. The cost? £8 return.)

The Grand Prix was contested over 500 kilometres, or forty laps of the combined road and banked course, and this time chicane corners were introduced; an announcement by the Mercédès-Benz team described the course as 'obstructed by obstacles in order to minimize the danger which the superior performance of the Mercédès-Benz cars contains for its rivals'! The entries included teams of the fabulous Mercédès-Benz and Auto-Union cars from Germany, two red Scuderia Ferrari Alfa-Romeos (these being the new 4-litre straight-eight cars with normal suspension), Robert Benoist in a long 3.8-litre Bugatti, and two Scuderia Subalpina Maseratis. The new vee-eight power units were unfortunately not ready for the latter entrants. The only non-starter was the ill-fated French SEFAC.

The race was run in hot weather, and the women spectators wore gay summer frocks. Benoist did a lap of the *Piste de Vitesse* to warm up the Bugatti. As the starter's flag fell, von Stuck's Auto-Union streaked into the lead, but after a lap it was Nuvolari in front in an Alfa-Romeo, Stuck a few yards in arrears on the high banking.

It became an Italian-German battle again, for behind the Auto-Union came Varzi's sister car, then Caracciola's Mercédès-Benz, Fagioli's Mercédès-Benz, and Chiron's Alfa-Romeo.

Big, excellent score boards showed the crowd how the race was shaping. Varzi was soon in his pit, but Nuvolari held his lead on the second lap. Now Caracclola was up in third place behind Stuck, and Chiron was fourth, having moved up two places. A nice touch was showing the numbers of the leaders on the scoreboards against the national racing colours; ltaly's white numbers on a red background, Germany's red numbers on a white ground, France's number white on blue.

After three laps the board showed a red, a white, a red, four whites and then a blue background in that order, the last for the veteran Benoist who has passed Zehender's Maserati on the banking. Alas, his car's bonnet blew up and jackknifed, and Benoist had some nasty moments, swerving wildly before managing to fling it away.

Now Caracciola took the lead at Les Biscornes. The Mercédès-Benz was one second ahead of Nuvolari's Alfa-Romeo, and set a new lap record of 84.56mph. But the wiry Tazio Nuvolari wasn't having this, and, as Chiron ran into trouble, the other Alfa-Romeo regained its lead. With all this excitement and anticipation — an ltalian victory would have been popular — almost unnoticed the Auto-Unions and the lone Bugatti developed serious mechanical trouble. The Maseratis were too slow and Sommer lost much time at his pit.

But Nuvolari stayed ahead, five seconds, seven seconds, eight seconds in front of the three Mercédès-Benz as the laps were ticked off. Few cars could survive a race when dogged by the entire Mercédès-Benz team, and perhaps the crowd was hardly surprised to hear on the loudspeakers that Nuvolari had slowed by Les Quatre Bornes. The Alfa-Romeo crawled to its pit, the mechanics jacked up the back axle, spun the wheels, and agreed with the driver that the transmission had failed.

This happened before half-distance; with Nuvolari's retirement, much of the interest of the Grand Prix waned. At 150 kilometres the little Italian had averaged 83.4mph, but now team manager Neubauer slowed his cars, and at half-distance Fagioli led at an average speed of 81.7mph, followed by his team-mates Caracciola and von Brauchitsch. Zehender's Maserati held fourth place.

In due time all three Mercédès-Benz cars came in for routine pit-stops, and work was done on the engine of Fagioli's car. This Mercédes-Benz was in real trouble, and only retained its third place because the Maserati stopped at its pit for ten minutes. However, the other Mercédès-Benz drivers had resumed their correct stations; Rudi Caracciola ahead of von Brauchitsch.

So the French Grand Prix ran its course with the two leading German cars never again challenged and the rest of the field in dire trouble. In the end, Zehender's Maserati gained a lap on Fagioli's sick Mercédès to finish third, two laps behind the leaders. Varzi's Auto-Union was fifth and Sommer's Maserati sixth; both five laps in arrears of Caracciola, who won at an average speed of 77.4mph, leading von Brauchitsch over the line by half a second.

John Cobb, Rose-Richards and Charlie Dodson had been notably successful on the Utah salt flats with the big Napier-Railton, taking the world hour record at 152.7mph and the twenty-four-hours at 137.4mph, so George Eyston bestirred himself. He decided to challenge the world forty-eight-hour record at Montlhéry, using the well-streamlined 2-litre Hotchkiss. Unfortunately, Montlhéry was getting bumpy in places, and trouble was experienced with the car's tail coming adrift. The full-length run had to be abandoned, but not before the 500-kilometre, 500-mile, 1000-kilometre, 1000-mile, three hour and six-hour Class records had been taken at speeds of 112.37 to 109.5mph.

Meanwhile, Gwenda Stewart was over at Brooklands meeting Kay Petre's vee-twelve Delage in a match race with the Derby Special, which she lost. A few days later, however, she recaptured the Brooklands Ladies' lap record at 135.95mph, a figure which will stand for ever.

What with Eyston going out to Utah with his new Rolls-Royce-powered record-breaker, Gwenda going to Brooklands, and poor Eldridge dying of pneumonia in a London nursing home, there was relatively little going on at the French track in 1935. Gwenda spoke of trying for the Class F hour record with her road-racing, four-cylinder Derby-Maserati with the Maserati 4C engine, a car which exists to this day in fine fettle in England, but no news of the attempt had been received by the end of the year.

Mrs Stewart, Fred Cann, and the Derby-Maserati in 1935.
(The Autocar)

George Eyston
attempts to
break the world
forty-eight-hour
record in the
2-litre Hotchkiss;
1935. (The
Autocar)

The 1935 French Grand Prix: Caracciola comes through a chicane with his Mercédès-Benz. (The Autocar)

Chapter 13

1936: the Grand Prix of the sports cars

During 1935 records for diesel-engined cars were officially recognised. R J Munday put a Perkins oil engine into one of the old 'flat-iron' Thomas Specials, supercharging it for the short distance runs, and established the first such record at Brooklands.

George Eyston, who may have had an inkling that sooner or later diesel records would have a proper class to themselves, naturally got busy. He had been occupied at Utah previously with his aero-engined car 'Speed of the Wind', and in this he installed a diesel engine with which to attempt short distance, compression-ignition (ci) engine records on Pendine Sands in Wales.

He then brought out the AEC diesel-powered saloon which previously had had to be content to demonstrate its speed unofficially, and drove it at Montlhéry to collect more ci-class records over longer distances. Never content to do things by halves, Eyston set out to take as many records as possible in the new class, the AEC saloon, with London omnibus-type engine and Chrysler chassis, driven on and on into the hours of darkness. For this attempt Eyston enlisted the aid of Albert Denly and Tommy Wisdom. The AEC duly raised Munday's records for fifty-kilometres, fifty-miles, 100-kilometres, 100-miles and one-hour at average speeds of 98.685, 101.252, 101.831, 102.956, and 103.014mph respectively, the driver comfortably esconced within the closed body. The car went on to establish the 200-kilometre record at 103.218mph, the 200-mile record at 103.021mph, and the three-hour record at 97.647mph before disaster struck ...

It was now dark, and the AEC'S headlamps were ablaze, red lanterns picking out the edge of the track. Denly was driving when

144

the big saloon swerved and shot up the banking, nearly going over the edge. Fortunately, it came down again, stopping in a shower of sparks. A front wheel had come off, leaving Denly with very little he could do to control the car.

Meanwhile, a more lighthearted form of motoring activity had been taking place at Montlhéry. Following Brooklands practice, the Track Manager, Letorey, had had the Monte Carlo Rally 'wiggle-woggle' test marked out so that competitors in the forthcoming event could practice. Using ordinary – as distinct from rally – cars, such celebrated competitors as Mlle Helle-Nice, Mlle Lamberjack, Mme Mareuse, Mlle Hustinx, Mme de Bourbon, Mme Masinovitch, Stoffel, Wagner, Lahaye, Quatresous and others whose very names epitomise the romance of the pre-war Monte Carlo Rallies, tried hard but had to concede to Vasselle, who managed a time of fifty-nine seconds in his Hotchkiss.

Early in 1936 Eyston was awarded the Segrave Trophy in recognition of his long succession of scientifc and eminently successful record attempts. It was as inevitable as sunrise and sunset that George should repair the rather tired chassis of the AEC and, finding Albert Denly in no way demoralised by his previous alarming experience, go out again at Montlhéry.

The pair set ci-class records for fifty-kilometres at 98.75mph, 1000-miles at 97.89mph, 2000-miles at 96.42mph, 3000-kilometres at 96.53mph, the twelve-hour record at 98.0,5mph, and the diesel twenty-four-hour record at 94.99mph, before Eyston went off to Pendine with another diesel-engined monster.

The AEC had a long, slender, streamlined saloon body with nose cowling now cut away round the radiator header tank, and two headlamps set close together within the base of the cowl.

It was becoming obvious that other places more suitable than Montlhéry for brief bursts or sustained high speed were being used for record attempts, so that record-breaking activity was diminishing at the Paris track. Gwenda Stewart – having been persuaded to try her hand at road-racing (for which the 1½-litre Derby-Maserati was built) – offered her famous Derby Special for sale in April 1936 for £1200, including innumerable spares, patterns, drawings, and so forth.

Eyston, out at Utah, set the ci fastest ever record to 158.87mph over the kilometre, using a Ricardo engine (which is now an exhibit in the Montagu Motor Museum at Beaulieu) in his front-wheel-drive chassis. (This has nothing whatsoever to do with Montlhéry, other than to emphasise how very fast even ci-engined record cars were going, and how impossible it had become to challenge any of the shorter records on a banked track.)

But if record attempts were now few and far between, Montlhéry still had the French Grand Prix race as a major attraction.

In 1936 Europe was in the doldrums and strikes in France threatened this classic event, which, to encourage entries, had been reduced to the status of a sports car race. Nevertheless, a good and open contest resulted. Indeed, *The Autocar* referred to it as: 'All That a Race Should Be'.

The race was run on the last Sunday in June over the full road-and-track circuit, and the entry list was an interesting one. Ettore Bugatti had prepared a team of his twin-cam, 3.3-litre cars. Their tanklike bodies had spatted rear wheels, and the streamlining was so effective that extension tubes had to be provided for jacking up the cars. The cockpits were open, but with the passenger side faired over, and the driver was protected by a small aero-screen. Talbot and Delahaye also put in a strong entry, which was sufficient to draw a good assembly of French spectators.

The race was over 1000 kilometres, divided into three separate classes of up to 2-litres, 3- to 4-litres and over 4-litres. The cars had to be painted in their national colours and a 'Le Mans' start was employed. Race day dawned fine with the expectancy of heat later. When the drivers were released, Lehoux, in a British Lagonda, and Dreyfus with a Talbot, were the first to pull away, followed by Benoist's Bugatti. Benoist was in at his pit almost at once with plug trouble, but Wimille took the lead in another of the very fast and impressive-looking cars, the wings of which were in dark blue, and bonnet, tail and cockpit in light blue.

*The French Grand Prix of 1936: Leoz's Lagonda; Benoist's
Bugatti, and Zehender's Delahaye. (*The Autocar*)*

The Talbots hung on to Wimille's Bugatti until they, too,
experienced trouble, coming in misfiring badly. Apparently, their
carburation was amiss on this warm morning, so after a tenth
of the race had been run, Wimille's Bugatti led from Zehender's
Delahaye, with Dreyfus' Talbot third but likely to be overtaken
at any moment by Veyron's Bugatti. Sure enough, before 150
kilometres Dreyfus had stopped; the order at the head of the field
was Bugatti, Delahaye, Bugatti, Delahaye, Delahaye, Bugatti.

In the 2-litre class the 328 BMWs were showing their worth
in no uncertain fashion, Henne's not only leading those of Roth
and Aldington (who sold them in England), but being something
of a menace to the far larger Delahayes. Behind these light six-
cylinder German cars ran a string of Rileys; slower, but steady.
Arthur Fox was perturbed at the sprint racing tactics which
Lehoux was adopting in the 4½-litre Lagonda, which was hard
on its brakes to say the least. But this kept Lehoux comfortably in
front of the Hudsons and another Lagonda, driven by Leoz, in the
same class.

Wimille's efficient Bugatti was also going very fast for this stage of the long race, setting a lap record of 81.07mph, then 81.23mph, but Cadot's Talbot had retired already, its fuel tank leaking hopelessly. At quarter-distance the first three were Wimille, Zehender and Veyron, but, as predicted, Lehoux's Lagonda had had to have all its brake shoes changed, which forced it right back. Trintignant's multi-carburetter Hudson now headed this class.

Henne, too, was out, his BMW losing all oil pressure, so it was Trevoux in a Riley who led the 2-litre category.

The race looked pretty safe for Bugatti, especially when Zehender's Delahaye came in for Brunet to take over and lost four minutes at the pits. However, in motor racing you can never be absolutely sure of yourself, and when the '3.3' Bugattis came in for their routine pit-stops the wheels, on these elaborately-streamlined cars, took a considerable time to change, and the engines were reluctant to re-start. The brake shoes had also to be changed.

The upshot was that Delahayes took the first four places in the main race, although the Talbots were now running properly and closing fast, whilst the second BMW, after Henne's retirement, had caught and passed the Riley to lead the 2-litre class.

Among the small cars Donald Barnes had his Singer in front of the Fiats, the Bugattis had got going again, and the irrepressible Sommer did his utmost to get amongst the Talbots and Delahayes.

Half-distance found the Delahayes still in the four leading places but strongly challenged by the Bugattis, though the Delahaye drivers had changed places. The BMW/Riley battle continued, the rest of the Rileys remaining in steady formation, but the Barnes/Bicknell Singer lost a lot of time with gear selector maladies. As trouble spread to Divo's Delahaye, to Benoist's Bugatti, and to the Hudson, the Sommer Bugatti crept ever closer to the leading Delahayes. Earl Howe was sharing a Marendaz Special with Tommy Wisdom in the 2-litre class, but stub-axle trouble held them back very badly.

The BMWs, pressed hard by the relentless Riley team, were long delayed at the pits, to the benefit of the British cars. Gradually Wimille worked his Bugatti closer until, at the 650 kilometre mark, he passed the fastest Delahaye at Les Biscornes. But this was an age of pit-work, and the 1936 French Grand Prix was no exception. When Wimille stopped he did so for a long time, so the Delahaye was able to regain the lead; moreover, when its turn came to re-fuel it got away still ahead of the Bugatti. Williams, in the second Bugatti, set the lap record to a furious 82.67mph.

A Hudson ran out of fuel, became ditched, was re-started by some spectators, but soon caught fire and was burnt out, the resultant smoke making an unpleasant hazard for other drivers. Nor was the Trintignant Hudson any longer healthy. At 750 kilometres Paris' Delahaye led from the Brunet/Zehender Delahaye, the Wimille/Sommer Bugatti now a bad third.

Von der Becke and Dobbs led the 2-litre class with their Riley, and a Lagonda led the over-4-litres cars. The Lehoux Lagonda was out, *sans* brakes, as was the Seaman/Clarke Aston Martin.

The crowd now clocked the ever-closing gap between the Delahayes and the fast-driven Bugatti, which took the lead again just after 800 kilometres. The question was, would it need another tyre change? The onlookers watched, rather as we at Goodwood watched Stirling Moss' Ferrari in the 1960 TT. Nor could the Talbots be disregarded; they were coming up fast.

Further pit-stops were not necessary, so the Bugatti won, no fewer than four Delahayes following it over the finishing line.

The results were:

1st   Wimille/Sommer (Bugatti) 77.8.5mph
2nd   Paris/Mongin (Delahaye)
3rd   Zehender/Brunet (Delahaye)
4th   Schell/Carrière (Delahaye)
5th   Perrot/Dhome (Delahaye)
6th   Veyron/Williams (Bugatti)

7th	Villeneuve/Viale (Delahaye)
8th	Helde/Nime (Talbot)
9th	Dreyfus/Bradley (Talbot)
10th	Morel/Chinetti (Talbot)
11th	Danniel/Marie (Delahaye)
12th	Divo/Girod (Delahaye)

2-litre Class:

1st	Trevoux/Maclure (Riley) 68.38mph (14th overall)
2nd	Von der Becke/Dobbs (Riley) (15th overall)
3rd	Paul/Sebilleau (Riley) (16th overall)

2.4-litre Class:

1st	Wimille/Sommer (Bugatti) 77.85mph
2nd	Paris/Mongin (Delahaye)
3rd	Zehender/Brunet (Delahaye)

4-litre Class:

| 1st | Leoz (Lagonda) 64.54mph |
| 2nd | Trintignant (Hudson) (19th overall) |

Soon after this enthralling Grand Prix Robert Benoist took one of the tank-bodied 3.3-litre Bugattis out on the banked circuit and set the Class C 100-kilometre record to the impressive speed of 130.88mph. Gwenda Stewart had failed to sell the famous Derby Special, the price now dropped to £750, to include spares but not various drawings which gave clues to making this remarkable single-seater even faster.

Benoist, aided by Veyron, then set the Class C 200-mile record at 127.73mph; the 500-kilometres at 125.49mph; the three-hours at 125.99mph; the 500-miles at exactly 127mph; the 1000-kilometres at 126.41mph (interesting comparison with the GP-winning average speed), and the six-hours at 126.91mph. All this with a Bugatti of GP type, but non-supercharged. Later, the pair also secured the Class C twelve-hour and twenty-four-hour

Two of the Bugattis at the pits during the 1936 French Grand Prix. (The Autocar)

records at 123.93mph and 123.27mph, as well as five intermediate class records: an astonishing demonstration of prolonged high-speed reliability in a Grand Prix-type car.

Then, in Class E, the Dutchman Hertsberger — who liked to paint his cars bright orange — used his K3 MG Magnette to break the 500-kilometre record at 108.89mph, the 200-mile record at 109.74mph, and the three-hour record at 108.49mph, which showed that even 1100cc racing cars were both very fast and tolerably reliable by 1936.

Finally, as the year ended, the French government awarded Gwenda Stewart its medal for outstanding physical prowess, the King's consent being required before it was granted to her.

She was the only racing driver ever to be so honoured.

A Hudson burns during the French Grand Prix of 1936. (The Autocar)

Chapter 14

1937: Bugatti scoops the pool

The 1937 season at Montlhéry opened with two exciting items of news. The first was that the French government, probably alarmed by the effect French labour troubles were having on her motor industry, put up a fund of one million francs to encourage motor racing, out of which a prize of 200,000 francs was offered for the first French car to average 90mph for 200 kilometres of the complete road-and-track circuit before the end of March. A similar sum was offered for a similar feat if accomplished by the end of August. Then, Gwenda Stewart married Douglas Hawkes, designer of Derby cars, and announced that they would continue to live at Montlhéry.

On the racing side it was announced that the French Grand Prix would again be for sports cars, and would be held at the Paris track. The event was open to any unsupercharged sports car from one to 4½-litres capacity, but AIACR bodies with two doors were specified, and whereas the smallest cars must not weigh less than 480kg, the big fellows were required to tip the scales at at least 1019kg. The race distance, alas, had been reduced from 1000 kilometres to 500 kilometres, and refuelling was not allowed. The *Coupe de la Commission Sportive* race was to be run separately, and was for cars of near-catalogue specification like those qualifying for the TT. The distance was 300 kilometres and engines were limited in size to 750-1500cc.

By March, there was a plan afoot to run an international match race between France and England, the idea originating among competitors at Montlhéry. Five cars from each country were to be involved in a race in heats over 100 kilometres of the road course, and a handicap. Madame Itier, a well-known lady motorist, came to England and animated discussions ensued, but nothing came of the idea.

The 200,000 franc prize offered by the French government deprived British spectators of seeing Wimille's Bugatti run in the Empire Trophy Race at Donington, because he was busy at Montlhéry in pursuit of this reward. His first run had ended in back-axle failure, but he tried again, driving a Type 59 3.3-litre GP Bugatti, averaging the spectacular speed of 91.13mph for the 200 kilometres, which was only fractionally below the lap record set by Brauchitsch's Mercédès-Benz. Wimille also raised the record to 92.44.mph.

A similar award was made subsequently to Delahaye, after its new 4½-litre vee-twelve Grand Prix car had averaged 91.07mph over 200 kilometres of the road circuit. The driver was René Dreyfus.

George Eyston came into the picture again, using the diesel AEC saloon, which, with Denly driving alternate spells, set the ci fifty-kilometre record at 106.27mph, and the hour record at 105.59mph. On a fresh run, the pair broke the 1000-kilometre record at 98.51mph, the 1000-mile record at 99.10mph, the twelve-hour record at 99.03mph, and the twenty-four-hour record at 97.05mph. Other records, in Class C, were broken by a team of lady drivers – Mesdames Helle-Nice, Siko, des Forest and Descollas – using a Ford V8-engined Matford, which took honours from 15,000 kilometres upward from the big Austin that had held them since 1934, ending its run after three days at 84.24mph. Finally, the ladies seem to have bagged two world records, and altogether kept going for ten days at 88mph, lapping at nearly 90mph.

Before the summer was out Dreyfus had been at Montlhéry testing the impressive new vee-twelve 4½-litre sports Delahaye, with high wings, prior to the Picardy Grand Prix.

The French Grand Prix in June got off to a late start owing to a dispute. Divo and Comotti in their Talbots, and Dreyfus in the vee-twelve Delahaye, had driven round the *Piste de Vitesse* to warm the transmissions, but other competitors were not allowed to do so. A one minute penalty was suggested for the drivers who had driven round, which caused Sommer, Chiron and Divo to refuse to race. The matter was sorted out satisfactorily in the end, and the race, which had thus earned an English headline 'Strike Spreads to French Motor Racing', duly began, after Sommer irritably skidded his Talbot into position.

It was a poor field which roared away for, in the absence of the works Bugattis and the new Delage (which had crashed badly in practice), only four 4-litre, six-cylinder Talbots, the three works Delahayes, three independent Delahayes and de Sauge's 3.3-litre Bugatti remained.

The Talbots snatched a good lead from the start, and were never caught. The Bugatti was soon at its pit, then Chaboud's ugly semi-streamlined Delahaye stopped. Dreyfus was merely trying out the new Delahaye, which lost a great deal of time over plug changes and carburetter adjustment.

Sommer and Comotti, however, were making an exciting fight for the lead, the latter getting round at 83.07mph, then at 83.19mph; a sports car lap record. This put Comotti ahead of Sommer, but the latter responded by pushing the record first to 83.49, then to 83.59mph. These two duellists were followed by Chiron and Divo, also in Talbots. Only Carrière and Laury Schell were in the running with Delahayes.

The pit-stops of the leading pair, at nineteen and twenty laps respectively, were crucial. Comotti closed right up on Sommer before stopping, causing him to overshoot his pit. It took a considerable time to have all four wheels changed and water put in the radiator. Sommer was calmer, helping his mechanics, but he re-started with the jacks still under the wheels and, as these were released, dragged a jack along the track for many yards.

Sommer led at half-distance – 250 kilometres or twenty laps – at 82.99mph, Chiron now second and Divo third. Chiron led after the pit-stops, completing a lap at 84.45mph, but was due in, and after twenty-five laps his Talbot came to rest. Only the back tyres were changed, which saved many seconds, and he retained his lead over Sommer by about four seconds. For some time Sommer – crouched almost out of sight in the cockpit of his blue Talbot – kept closing the gap, but the wily Chiron increased his speed on the thirty-second lap, leaving the sports car record at 84.83mph. Then Sommer's Talbot suddenly began to make dreadful noises. It pitted; the duel had ended. Chiron secured a very popular victory, the results being:

1st	Chiron (Talbot)	82.47mph
2nd	Comotti (Talbot)	81.71mph
3rd	Divo (Talbot)	81.14 mph
4th	Carrière (Delahaye)	
5th	Sommer (Talbot)	
6th	Chaboud (Delahaye)	

This was the last occasion that this long-established classic race was run at Montlhéry.

The small car race had begun at 9am that morning and was not particularly interesting. Arthur Dobson's TT-type four-cylinder, 1½-litre Riley won easily, followed home by three four-cylinder Rileys driven by Frenchmen. Dobson's car was a 1936 model, painted green, whereas the French-entered Nines had blue, specially streamlined Pourtout bodies with enclosed rear wheels. Dobson's best lap was at 72.20mph. The results were:

1st	Dobson (1½-litre Riley)	70.12mph
2nd	Contet (Riley Nine)	69.08mph
3rd	Forestier (Riley Nine)	68.61mph
4th	Lapchin (Riley)	
5th	Girard Cabantous (Chenard-Walcker)	
6th	Camerano (Simca-Fiat)	
7th	Maillard-Brune (Simca-Fiat)	

The strenuous Bol d'Or twenty-four-hour race, formerly held in the forest of St Germain, came to Montlhéry's road circuit in

157

1937, the winner — Rigoulot — covering 1332 miles at 54.72mph in a Chenard-Walcker. Second place was taken by Cabantous in a similar car, Maillard-Brune coming third in a Riley.

Very little more activity was seen at Montlhéry during the remainder of 1937. Eyston was away at Utah preparing to break the world Land Speed Record, but the 1700cc diesel-engined Yacco made history at the Paris track by taking normal, as distinct from ci, Class records for 20,000-kilometres and on up to eight days, at an average speed of 68.06mph. Maillard-Brune, Gordini, Viale

Two of the Talbots competing in the 1937 French Grand Prix. (The Autocar)

and Alin used a small Simca-Fiat to take the Class 5000-kilometre record at well over 60mph.

Then Major 'Goldie' Gardner, returning from a record onslaught on the Darmstadt road, decided there were some records his ex-Horton, Robin Jackson-tuned MG Magnette could take at Montlhéry. He duly annexed the Class G five- and ten-mile and five- and ten-kilometre records at speeds of 129.98, 129.43, 130.52 and 129.79mph, which was very fast for a 1100cc car.

In July 1937, the track was occupied by Marchand and his co-drivers, who, with a 1.7-litre Yacco Speciale, set international compression ignition records of 5000-kilometres at 70.02mph to eight-days (13,090 miles, 1730 yards) at 68.18mph (109.73kph).

Louis Chiron, winner of the 1937 French Grand Prix.
(The Autocar)

Arthur Dobson's Riley (right) is followed by Gordini's and Camerano's Simca-Fiats in the 1½-litre race which preceded the 1937 French Grand Prix. (The Autocar)

Chapter 15

1938-39: the end of an era

By 1938 Montlhéry was in the doldrums, kept going mainly by the great enthusiasm of the track's General Manager, Letorey. Events like the French Grand Prix had gone elsewhere; record attempts had been transferred to temporarily closed motor roads, or the salt flats of Utah to cope with the greatly increased speed of the cars: routine testing apart, there was far less activity at the Paris Autodrome.

The French Independent Drivers' Club realized that, to help the situation, the best solution would be to introduce handicap races such as those which had kept Brooklands active since 1907; events for all types of cars, even obsolete models. Handicap races had never been acceptable to the French, and the plan did not reach fruition, but a series of short races did, in fact, take place, consisting of heats and finals.

In these races Forestier's Riley won the 1½-litre class, Hertberger's Aston Martin the 2-litre class, and Lebègue's Talbot the over 2-litre category.

The Bol d'Or twenty-four-hour endurance race was again held over the road course, and was won by Gordini's Fiat (which covered 1522 miles at 63.38mph) from De Burnay's MG and Polledry's Aston Martin.

Chiron and Raph were reduced to racing on bicycles, but on 11 September a twelve-hour race for sports cars was held at Montlhéry, which was won by youthful Rene Lebègue and veteran André Morel, who shared a Darracq. They averaged 75.69mph to win a first prize of 10,000 francs, Villeneuve and Biolay finishing some way behind in a Delahaye. Mesdames Roulant and Itier were third in another Delahaye. The 3-litre class was won at 61.98mph

161

by Mestivier and Mme Roux driving an Amilcar; the 2-litre category was a victory for Haeberle and Glockner at the wheel of an interesting diesel-engined Hanomag, which maintained an average speed of 52.58mph for the twelve hours, and Ferry and Noireaux won the 1½-litre class in a Riley from another Riley driven by Vernet and de Bodard, the winning car averaging 59.67mph. A Simca-Fiat handled by Molinari and Allain was victorious in the 1100cc class at a speed of 60.57mph, and the 750cc class was won by a smaller Simca-Fiat shared between Lapchin and Plantivaux, which averaged 52.72mph.

There might well have been more excitement at Montlhéry during 1938 had not that inveterate record-breaker, George Eyston, been away at Utah duelling with John Cobb for the 'fastest-ever' record.

The last season of competition before the outbreak of war saw activity at Montlhéry early in March, when the Paris-St Raphael Women's Rally commenced with a special test at the track. Then the latest 3-litre vee-sixteen GP Talbot arrived for test, achieving speeds of a little over 140mph, although its sponsors expected it eventually to be good for 190mph.

Racing still took place at Montlhéry; a series of short events similar to those which constituted the BARC's main activity at Brooklands, organized by the Independent Drivers' Club.

At the meeting of 7 May 1939, proceedings opened with the Sporting Committee Cup Race for sports cars, which Gordini won by a narrow margin in his 1100cc Simca-Fiat from Brunot's 1½-litre Riley, these two winning on general classification two-and-a-half minutes ahead of Herkuleyn's MG. The Coupe de Paris Race, for racing cars, resulted in a grand ding-dong battle between Wimille in a 4.9-litre GP Bugatti and Sommer's 2.9-litre Alfa-Romeo. At half-distance Wimille led by two seconds, with Lebègue and Carrière going well behind the two of them in their Darracqs, a string of Delahayes and Darracqs following behind. Sommer then fell back a few yards and Wimille won by about ten seconds. This hectic race lasted three quarters of an hour.

Lebègue came home third, his Darracq only thirty-six seconds behind Sommer.

The day's sport concluded with a rally which terminated at Montlhèry, the winner driving a Fiat 500; Contet's Delahaye was placed second, and Sommer's Alfa-Romeo third. Rainer Dorndorf and Miss Patten had arrived from England with a Peugeot, which finished second in the 2-litre Class.

An event of considerable moment followed these races, for Raymond Sommer had realized how fast his Tipo 308C 1938 2.9-litre straight-eight Alfa-Romeo was, so used it during the afternoon to challenge Gwenda Stewart's Montlhéry lap record, which she held in the Derby Special at 147.79mph. Sommer put in three very fast laps of Montlhéry's banked circuit, and, on its fourth lap, the Alfa-Romeo clocked 148.4mph, a new lap record which has never been beaten. Actually, it appears that the run was hand-timed, not recorded electrically, and there was some doubt about the validity of Sommer's record ...

How did Mrs Hawkes (*née* Gwenda Stewart) react? She said that she thought if she had a 2-litre engine in the Derby Special (which was of a mere 1.6 litres capacity) she could improve on the Alfa-Romeo's lap speed.

The future of Montlhéry was at this time uncertain, rumour suggesting that the Autodrome might be acquired by the French Ministry of National Defence. War clouds were gathering.

The Bol d'Or, that arduous, long distance race with only one driver permitted per car, was held over Montlhéry's road circuit for the third time. The winner was Contet in an Aston Martin which covered 1433 miles, at an average speed of 59.60mph. Debille's Fiat was second, and Guenin's Bugatti third.

Drivers had for some time been turning their attention to seeing how far they could go in an hour in more or less standard sports cars, and at Montlhéry Robert Benoist — soon to die so tragically in the war — covered 113 miles in sixty minutes at the wheel of a normal supercharged, 3.3-litre Type 57C Bugatti Galibier-bodied saloon, its fastest lap completed at a speed of 121mph.

Another run in this category seen at Montlhéry during 1939 was made by the 4¼-litre Bentley Continental saloon driven by Bentley's Paris manager, which averaged 107.42mph, with a best lap of 110.04mph. Fuel consumption came out at 12.2mpg.

The sands now ran out, and racing gave way to war. The Coupe de Paris meeting and the 12 Heures de Paris race were abandoned. Montlhéry was taken over by the military and its manager, Robert Letorey, joined his regiment. Many well-known French racing drlvers, including Trevoux, Dreyfus, Sommer, Chiron and Wimille, also joined the army, while Roger Loyer, Louis Villeneuve, Girard Cabantous and Vernet joined the *Armie de l'Air*.

It was the end of an era. But, whereas the Second World War sounded the death-knell of the Brooklands motor course in England, Montlhéry Autodrome was to survive.

Chapter 16

1947-53: Montlhéry redivivus

With the war over and Hitler exterminated, Montlhéry gradually got back into its stride, extensively used by the French motor industry for testing purposes of many kinds, and for a resumption of races and record attempts.

Activity resumed late in 1947. First of all Alan Hess, then PRO to the Austin Motor Company, hit upon the idea of challenging other makes of cars to a series of performance tests against two of the cars in the Austin range. George Eyston was still associated with Montlhéry; so much so that he flew over ready to drive the two A40s and an Austin Sixteen against all comers. However, as the Austin challenge had been kept secret until the last minute, there were no takers and the plot fizzled out.

At Paris Salon time a streamlined 1100cc Darlmat-Peugeot saloon broke the Class G 1000-mile, 2000-kilometre and twelve-hour records, held by an Amilcar since 1933, at 89.19, 90.13, and 90.0mph respectively, averaging 26½mpg for the duration of its successful onslaught.

Then Austin felt it had better put up some figures to support its unaccepted challenge, and one of the new A40 saloons lapped at 72mph, disposing of the standing start kilometre in 47.4sec, while the Austin Sixteen saloon lapped at 75mph and covered the standing start kilometre in 45.2sec.

To enliven the period of the Paris Motor Show the Coupe du Salon race was held at Montlhéry, within easy reach of Paris. In 1947 it took the form of a 187 mile free-for-all race over the short 7.5-kilometre road course. Fourteen cars started and Louis Chiron led for a time, until his 4½-litre Talbot succumbed to transmission failure. This enabled Yves Girard Cabantous to put Lord Selsdon's

4½-litre Talbot into the lead. After Sommer had blown up Ruggeri's two-stage, supercharged, sixteen-valve Maserati (with which he raised the lap record to 93.86mph), Cabantous won at 88.75mph, having driven for 2hr 6min 28sec. Chaboud, 1947 champion of France, was second in another 4½-litre Talbot; third place going to Pozzi's 3.6-litre Delahaye; fourth to Constantin's Delage; fifth to Louveau's Maserati; sixth to Rosier's Talbot; seventh to Robert's Cisitalia; eighth to Bonnet's little DB, and ninth place to Meyrat's Delahaye: a pretty good cross-section of motor racing as it was in France soon after the end of the Second World War. Incidentally, Cabantous won by the narrow margin of 4.7 seconds.

The first real excitement of 1948 was a ninety-four mile sports car race, which Meyrat's 3.6-litre Delahaye won at 76.8mph from Louveau, who now drove a 3-litre Delage with which he made fastest lap, at 87.05mph. A Riley won its Class, as Rileys had been wont to do before the war, and the Novices' Race, contested on the same day over forty miles, saw Simon's Lago-Talbot victorious at the reasonable speed of 70.68mph.

There followed the Paris Grand Prix over the short road circuit, twenty-three cars assembling to race for fifty laps, or a matter of 235 miles. Girard Cabantous made a good job of challenging the now-ageing Chiron, beating him by 2min 0.3sec, both drivers at the wheel of 4½-litre Talbots. Cabantous averaged 87.3mph. Rosier tried to pass Chiron but his Talbot broke down, allowing Chaboud to come in third three laps in arrears, in his 4½-litre Delahaye, the remaining places being occupied by Mairesse (3.6-litre Delahaye), Comotti (4½-litre Talbot), and the British driver P A T Garland (3-litre TT Delage).

On 12 September 1948 a more important race was held at Montlhéry, in the form of a twelve-hour sports car contest. Chinetti convincingly demonstrated the speed and reliability of the vee-twelve 2-litre sports Ferrari by driving it single-handed, with two pit-stops for fuel, to win at an average speed of 72.96mph. Besides his two refuelling stops the Italian got a fingernail caught in the horn-push, which somehow I find amusing. This necessitated another stop, and two more pit-stops were made for tyre changes; on one occasion, when a wheel refused to come off, the tyre was changed on the rim. Yet the Ferrari won easily!

Louveau and Brunet brought their 3-litre Delage home in second place and Folland and Ian Connell fnished third in their 1937 2-litre Speed Model Aston Martin. Cabantous' Talbot retired when a valve broke; the DB of Deutsch and Schell broke its front suspension; Rolt and Heath had the wheel nuts shear on their Alta; a Healey saloon developed engine trouble; Gerard's Delage caught fire, and Norman Black and Tommy Wisdom fell out with transmission failure on their Healey roadster. Quite a number of British drivers and cars competed, but Ian Metcalfe overturned his 8-litre Bentley 'The Whale' in practice. The class winners were:

750cc	Molinari/Prat (Simca)
1100cc	de Montrémy/Dussous (Monopole)
1500cc	Lachaize/Debille (DB)
2000cc	Chinetti (Ferrari)
3000cc	Louveau/Brunet (Delage)
over 3000cc	Brault/Marechal (Delahaye)

The Coupe du Salon race was held again at show-time. Leslie Johnson drove his E-type ERA but, as at Silverstone earlier, it retired after three laps with a split fuel tank, after making fastest practice lap at 97.76mph. Rosier's Lago-Talbot won, at 91.56mph, after a race lasting 2hr 3min 52.9sec. Levegh's Lago-Talbot was second and Cabantous' similar car third: Cabantous being 1948 Champion of France. Bira's Maserati went out with broken back axle radius rods. Reg Parnell's Maserati finished, but behind the Delahaye of Mairesse, the Maserati of Moore, and the Delahaye of Versini.

Then, during the period of the London Motor Show, the AC de France observed a fine run at Montlhéry by Tommy Wisdom, who drove a standard Healey saloon for one hour, covering 101.7

miles from a standing start and 103.76 miles with a flying start: excellent publicity for the little Warwick factory.

Finally, early in November, Chinetti broke the Class E 200-kilometre, 100-mile and one-hour records, driving an unsupercharged vee-twelve, 2-litre Ferrari. His speeds were, respectively, 126.229, 126.337, and 125.966mph.

At the very end of 1948, in training for an attempt on American Stock Car records at Indianapolis (which subsequently proved extremely successful), Alan Hess arrived at Montlhéry with Broom, Head Tester of the Austin Experimental Department, Boyle of SU Carburetters, 'Dunlop Mac' the famous tyre fitter, George Coats and Charles Goodacre, who were to act as co-drivers, and an Austin A90 Atlantic convertible. Among others, also present was Raleigh Appleby, there to help Broom, and Austin's official photographer, Ron Beach; quite an invasion, especially as Charles de Vries, Austin distributor in France, and many of his technicians and staff also looked in.

The Austin A90 was driven for forty-eight hours, in three hour spells, by Hess, Coats and Goodacre, covering 3725 miles at 77.7mph, in spite of unhurried pit-stops, during which carburation and other experiments were conducted.

The weather was cold, with frost. Hess tended to go to sleep between the grisly hours of 12.30 and 3.30am, but white and red lanterns helped to mark the track, and the Dunlop tyres stood up splendidly, changed at twenty-four hours as a precaution. In the last hour the Austin was driven harder than ever.

Early in February 1949 an unusual car arrived at Montlhéry. It consisted of a Delahaye chassis provided with a nicely streamlined, single-seater body whose features included a 'conning tower' screen round the cockpit and exposed wheels. Under the bonnet was a Manufacture des Armes diesel engine, normally found in tractors, a 4.9-litre horizontally-opposed two-stroke.

With this car F Lacour challenged the ci Class records held by George Eyston's AEC saloon. This AEC went extremely well, covering a lap of Montlhéry at 119.25mph and consuming fuel oil at the rate of over 20mpg. The hour record fell at 113.45mph, and on the way the fifty-kilometre, 100-kilometre, 100-mile and 200-kilometre Class records were broken, at respective speeds of 110.68, 111.73, 113.12 and 113.76mph.

In April the short road circuit was used for the Formula 1 Paris Grand Prix, which was won at 93.12mph by Etancelin in a 4½-litre Lago-Talbot, which did one lap at 96.93mph, a mere 0.83mph under the course lap record standing to the credit of Leslie Johnson's E-type ERA. Second place was taken by Grignard and Cabantous in another Lago-Talbot, and the Belgian driver Claes was third, also in a Lago-Talbot, followed home by Versini (3-litre Delage); Levegh (Lago-Talbot); Raph (3.6-litre Delahaye), and Roy Salvadori, driving a sixteen-valve Maserati once raced by Prince Bira. Englishman Lance Macklin had retired when his 6CL Maserati developed magneto trouble. Unfortunately, the spectators got out of hand and, in running across the course at the end of the race, caused Judet to crash in his Maserati.

There was a supporting small car race which Gordini's Simca won, at 76.82mph, from a Duval and a Peugeot.

Montlhéry was by now mainly occupied by manufacturers' test cars, but, in conjunction with the Paris Salon in October 1949, the GP du Salon was contested. It proved a dull race as a first lap accident eliminated three of the competitors, includng Peter Whitehead's Ferrari. Thereafter the event became a Talbot procession, Sommer winning at 92.38mph from Schell and Meyrat.

British motorcycle record-breakers made good use of Montlhéry before the end of 1949 (though motorcycle exploits are outside the scope of this book). Geoffrey Crossley crossed the Channel with his 1½-litre Grand Prix Alta and broke international Class F records, taking the fifty-kilometre record at 125.92mph, the fifty-mile record at 124.4mph, and the 200-kilometre record at 124.17mph. He had, however, merely to better speeds established in 1926 by the indomitable Ernest Eldridge and his Miller.

During the year 1950 there was more record-breaking activity at Montlhéry than had been the case since the track opened after the war. First of all, however, the Grand Prix de Paris was held on 29 April, with a Lago-Talbot again proving successful. It was driven by Georges Grignard and averaged 93.37mph, finishing four laps ahead of the second car home, which was Louis Gerard's Delage. The winner clocked 2hr 5min 38.8sec. The English HWMs were entered but those driven by Moss and Abecassis retired. Indeed, there was only one other finisher apart from the Lago-Talbot and the Delage; Versini's Delage.

The outcome of the 500cc or Formula 3 race was of great interest, as for the first time ever the French Panhard-powered flat-twin DBs met the English Coopers. British honour was upheld when Ken Carter's Cooper won after a drive of 48min 19sec, but Elie Bayol's DB chased the Cooper to very good effect, finishing only 18.1 seconds behind it. Coldham's Cooper was third.

The record breaking began towards the end of the year, when Alan Hess led a team comprising himself, Fisher, Jeavons and Walters, who drove a normal Austin A40 saloon to set up new Class F records over five days (7862.4 miles = 65.52mph); 15,000 kilometres (65.59mph); six days (9429.28 miles = 65.62mph); 10,000 miles (60.00mph), and seven days (10,009.4 miles = 59.58mph). This successful attempt on really long duration achievements robbed Citroën of records it had held for very many years.

A fairly standard four-cylinder, 1490cc Hansa Borgward aerodynamic two-seater, known as an Inka, then arrived at Montlhéry to attempt more normal Class F records, with drivers August Momberger, the pre-war Auto-Union racing driver, Heins Meir, Adolf Brudes, and Karl Schalzfell. Engine trouble intervened after 500 miles but the car returned later, the team hoping for the Class twenty-four-hour record.

Again trouble set in; this time a wheel broke up and the rear axle radius arms were damaged, but the old Eyston/Maclure records for 1000-miles (107.30mph), 2000-kilometres (105.47mph), and twelve-hours (105.48mph) still fell, at the speeds given within brackets; also the twenty-four-hour record at 94.45mph, and the forty-eight-hour record at 91.93mph.

A rather special Volkswagen next cleared up a lot of long duration Class G records formerly belonging to a Simca-Fiat; Muller, Glockner, von Hanstein and Polensky setting new fgures for 4000-kilometres (80mph), 3000-miles (72mph), 5000-kilometres (78.8mph), forty-eight-hours (78mph), 4000-miles (76.9mph), 5000-miles (77.1mph), three-days (77.2mph), and 10.000-kilometres (77mph). This Volkswagen used pump petrol and had a single carburetter, yet could lap at up to 85mph.

It is noticeable that no longer was there money in the kitty for constructing specialized record-breaking cars, the French luxury car industry very close to being in the doldrums, and the tendency now was to demonstrate the prowess of production cars with either standard or mildly-modified specifications.

With this in mind some Englishmen – Thompson, Charles Brackenbury, and Lance Macklin, aided by Bouchard – had the idea of trying to annex the 2000-mile, 3000-kilometre and twenty-four-hour Class D records, using an Aston Martin DB2. These records – belonging to the Yacco Citroën and established back in 1934 – were chosen as the Aston Martin should have little difficulty in breaking them. It was not to be, however, as first torrential rain and then dense fog hampered the run after a mere 500 miles had been covered. During this time the drivers were changed three times, in spite of which the car averaged 107mph for the first 100 miles. It averaged 103.79mph for 800 miles, after which the attempt was abandoned. The car never reappeared.

Towards the end of the 1950 season E Bayol, with a little DB, broke Class I records at Montlhéry from fifty- to 200-kilometres, including the hour record at approximately 87mph. A 745cc streamlined, two-seater, Le Mans Dyna-Panhard-engined DB driven by Bonnet, Bayol, Arnaud and Bouchard took Class H records, including the twelve-hour-record held previously by Eyston and Denly with the MG. The small French car covered 1254

Postwar emulator of the prewar Citroëns: a Simca on the banking.

Twenty-four hours at 107.46mph: Leslie Johnson in the XK120 Jaguar, 1950. (Jaguar Cars Ltd)

miles at 96.10mph in that time, taking, in addition, the Class records for three-hours (97.53mph); 500-miles (96.41mph); six-hours (96.78mph); 1000-kilometres (96.8cmph); 1000-miles (95.91mph), and 2000-kilometres (95.05mph).

Late in November 1950, two Kiefts of the kind built for Formula 3 racing were taken from England to Montlhéry to try their hand at record breaking. One was given a special single-overhead camshaft Norton engine for an onslaught on 500cc records, and the other a twin overhead camshaft 350cc engine for challenging records in Class J. Both engines had been prepared by the well-known tuner of racing motorcycles, Steve Lancefeld, and ran on methanol fuel.

The cars were normal versions with the long wheelbase of 7ft 6in but with long-range fuel tanks: drivers were J Neill, who owned one of the Kiefts, Ken Gregory (Moss' Manager), and Stirling Moss himself, who was racing an F3 Kieft.

The attempt was by no means free from trouble, the 350cc car developing crankpin trouble after 200 kilometres had been covered, while the larger-engined Kieft split its fuel tank after 200 miles, allowing fuel to pour on to the driver's legs, and finally ran its big-end. However, six international Class J and seven new international Class I records were broken. The former were for fifty-kilometres (78.44.mph); fifty-miles (78.75mph); 100-kilometres (79.08mph); 100-miles (79.62mph); 200-kilometres (77.11mph), and the hour (79.37mph): the latter covered fifty-kilometres (90.06mph); fifty-miles (90.63mph); 100-kilometres (90.87mph); 100-miles (91.40mph); 200-kilometres (88.60mph), and one hour (91.34mph). The 500cc records had belonged to Bayol's DB Panhard and were just over a year old; the Class J records had been set by the Vitesse Special, the HS, and the Gush, the last named having averaged 6.17mph less for the hour at Brooklands, way back in 1934.

There had been some anxiety about whether the Kiefts' rubber-in-torsion rear suspension was suitable for Montlhéry, but this department stood up well, in spite of a seven inch bounce over the rough parts of the track. The Dunlop tyres on the Class J car still showed the moulding seam after the hour run. Those on the Class I Kieft had lost only a millimetre or so thickness of rubber. These records were timed by hand. Had electrical timing apparatus been available, the Class J flying start ten-kilometre and ten-mile records – for which electrical timing was compulsory – would have been attempted. It is indicative of the complexity of the rules which govern world and international record breaking that Cyril Kieft was hopeful of being allowed to claim these short distance records without actually attempting them, on the grounds that his car had covered 100 miles from a standing start at a higher speed than the holder had managed over ten miles with a flying start. On the same basis, he expected to get the three-hour record, as the Kieft had covered a greater distance when it retired than the Vitesse Special had accomplished for the full duration. The *équipe* used Cyril Kieft's vee-eight Cadillac as a tender car, and amused themselves by thundering round the track in it; treatment which the car loudly protested after some fifteen laps!

Tony Crook indulged in a stunt on 12 October by driving from his showrooms at Caterham, Surrey, to Montlhéry, crossing the Channel in a Silver City Airways Bristol Freighter, lapping the track for an hour in his Bristol 401 saloon (covering 104.78 miles under official observation with two laps at 107.55mph), and returning to Caterham the same day.

Late in October a white Jaguar XK120 owned by Leslie Johnson arrived at Montlhéry and was driven under official observation for twenty-four hours by the owner and Stirling Moss. They coped with the thirteen hours of darkness using only the car's lighting system. The Jaguar averaged 107.46mph, several laps completed at 126mph, and 112.4 miles being put into the last hour of this demonstration (not record-breaking) run. Montlhéry was, indeed, popular for demonstrations such as those described, although apart from official confirmation of the speeds accomplished, these runs had no 'record' status.

The following year Tony Crook returned to the Paris track with a 2-litre 'Le Mans Replica' Frazer-Nash with which he averaged 120.47mph from a flying start in the course of a sixty-minute run while, with a 2-litre 'Mille Miglia' Frazer- Nash, he lapped at 121.8mph, covering ten kilometres at 120.5mph. Leslie Johnston tried the hour run in his XK120 Jaguar, now with C-type engine modifcations but running on 80-octane fuel as a sop to the road car aspect of these attempts. He averaged an excellent speed of 131.83mph, with a best lap of 134.43mph.

An interesting 1951 run was undertaken by H S F Hay, who, having taken part in the Le Mans twenty-four hour race in his Bentley Continental 'Corniche' saloon as part of a European holiday with his family, drove to the track and put in an hour at cruising rpm. He covered 106.84 miles. The Bentley had not been touched after the Le Mans race and was carrying fifty gallons of fuel, five gallons of oil, and a complete set of tools and equipment. Not even the tyres had been changed; the late Forrest Lycett undertook to kneel at the side of the track during the run to make sure that they were not about to fail. At the same time the American millionaire, Briggs Cunningham, attempted the hour run in his Le Mans Cunningham, but was forced to give up after three laps because the engine oil began to overheat.

Not much else of note occurred at Montlhéry in 1951 until October, when John Cooper and Bill Aston arrived with a specially-streamlined Cooper, thirsting for international Class I and J records; in fact, they were there to show Kieft which was the faster car. In this they were successful: John Cooper went out first, using a 350cc, single-cylinder JAP engine. He broke the Class J fifty-, 100- and 200-kilometre, and fifty- and 100-mile records, and also the hour record, at speeds of 90.62, 92.13, 91.98, 92.02, 91.80, and 90.27mph respectively. Bill Aston then used the same Cooper with a vee-twin 500cc JAP engine, cleaning up the same records in Class I at speeds of 99.30, 99.59, 99.13, 99.16, 99.41, and 99.41mph. It is interesting to find keen competition for record honours in the two smallest capacity classes (Class K, up to 250cc came later). It had become obvious that in the not-too-distant future the half-litre cars would achieve 100 miles in the hour, although in 1926, when Kaye Don set the initial Class I hour record at Brooklands with the Avon-JAP, this was established at a mere 62.2mph. Similarly, Gwenda Stewart set the first Class J hour record with the HS in 1928, at only 70.95mph.

Rather faster speeds had been achieved the month before at Montlhéry, when Mueller, Gloeckner, von Hanstein, Remelow and von Frankenberg took the Class G 500-mile, 1000-kilometre and six-hour records with a 1093cc Porsche, at 100.55, 101.23 and 101.17mph respectively, taking these records from the Eyston/ Denly Riley. The team came out again with a 1492cc Porsche and raised the Class F 2000-mile-to-seventy-two-hour records to speeds of from 98.82 to 94.66mph. The following month they set further Class F records in the 1492cc Porsche for 500- kilometres, 1000-kilometres and six-hours, at 116.88, 115.69 and 114.74mph.

Tony Crook had apparently gained useful experience from his hour run in the Frazer-Nash, for he returned to Montlhéry on 26 November and captured the international Class E 200-mile record, averaging 120.13mph with the 'Le Mans Replica' Frazer- Nash now stripped of road equipment. 123.55 miles were covered after an hour had elapsed – from a flying start – and the fastest lap was 123.92mph.

It is interesting to note that Crook had beaten a record which had stood intact to the credit of Jack Dunfee's Grand Prix Sunbeam for twenty-one years. There are no 'ifs' or 'buts' once a record has been officially confirmed, because it represents the highest speed or greatest distance achieved to-date in a given category. By 1951 the controlling body insisted that a one per cent margin of improvement over a previous record must be achieved to allow for any minor errors in time-keeping or track measurement. So Crook deserved his record, even if he had merely improved on a speed set up as long ago as 1930; it could be argued in his support that he was at the wheel of a catalogued sports car, whereas

Dunfee had driven a racing car, and a supercharged one at that. But, as I have said, in record breaking, 'ifs' and 'buts' must arise only as subsidiary thoughts, not detracting one iota from the achievements officially timed and recognized.

In addition, at the time of the Paris Salon, a team consisting of Cornu, Dussous, Guerne, Lienard, J Hemard, P Hemard and de Montrémy had broken Class H records for 2000-miles (86.41mph); 5000-kilometres (84.77mph); twenty-four-hours (86.46mph), and forty-eight-hours (78.78mph) driving a two-cylinder, 746cc Monopole-Poissy, a typical small French racing car of the period.

It was in 1952 that a truly outstanding feat was accomplished at Montlhéry. Leslie Johnson returned to the Paris track with a Jaguar XK120 coupé, LWK707, and, with Stirling Moss, Jack Fairman and Bert Hadley as his co-drivers, set out to average over 100mph for seven days and nights of continuous motoring. In this he was eminently successful. The run commenced on 5 August. The only trouble experienced by the Dunlop-shod Jaguar was a broken road spring, a reminder of Montlhéry's rough surface. This took some four hours to replace, and, as a spare spring was not carried on the car, no further world or international Class records could be attempted. Up to that time the amazing Jaguar – which was under the care of mechanics Thompson, Sutton and Potter – had broken the world and Class C seventy-two-hour records at 105.55mph, the Class C 10,000-kilometre record at 107.031mph, world and Class C four-day records at 101.17mph, world and Class C 15,000-kilometre records at 101.95mph, and world and Class C 10,000-mile records at 100.65mph.

Johnson drove for nine hours, refusing to involve the other drivers in added risk while the average speed had to be maintained on the broken spring. The Jaguar covered 16,851.73 miles at an average speed of 100.31mph, and Moss did one lap at 121.28mph. The car had a compression-ratio of 8:1 and ran on Shell petrol and Shell X100 lubricating oil. It was equipped with a radio by which the man at the wheel kept in touch with his depôt.

After this incredible endurance run was concluded the twin-

A week at over 100mph: the Jaguar XK120 fixed-head coupé on the banking at night in 1952. (Jaguar Cars Ltd)

cam engine was stripped at the Shell laboratory, and the following report issued —

'The general condition of the engine was excellent, and had the engine not been dismantled there was no apparent reason why it should not have given satisfactory service for many thousands of miles of normal hard driving. Crankshaft wear was so low that, in spite of the car having covered nearly 17,000 miles on the record run, plus just under 2000 miles previously, the crankshaft was still within production tolerances, and would have been passed by the inspection department for installation in a new car.

'Bore wear was not abnormal, showing a maximum of 3-3.5 thousandths at the top of the bore after a total mileage of about 18,708. All the pistons were in good condition apart from slight erosions on the top of one, while rings were bedded perfectly in the bore, and the absence of carbon deposits was particularly noticeable. The sump was free from sludge, as were also the camshaft covers. The cylinder head was virtually free from deposit, and the seats, both inlet and exhaust, were in a very satisfactory condition.

'All valves were seating perfectly, although slight pitting and blackening of the surface of the exhaust valves had occurred. The standard-type plugs, which had run the total distance, were in astonishingly good condition ... The rear axle cover-plate was removed and the crown wheel and differential examined. The axle was in perfect condition as far as could be seen, both faces of the crown wheel having an excellent finish, and the differential gears still showing some of the original machining marks.'

Nineteen-fifty-two was a season of long duration record attempts at Montlhéry. Apart from Jaguar's fine performance, a 1221cc Simca Aronde saloon, driven by a team composed of Gauthier, Quenlin, R Turcey, M Turcey, Duham, Toutain, Muzi, Dalem and Bergerot, went on and on, round and round the banked circuit, piling up international Class F records.

When this run finally concluded after eighteen days, twenty-seven records — from 10,000-miles and five-days upward — at speeds consistently around 72 and 73mph, stood to the credit of the Fiat-inspired French family saloon. The actual average speed for the full eighteen days, inclusive of depôt stops, was 72.89mph.

Brudes and Hartmann brought out a 1½-litre Borgward and broke Class F records for fifty-kilometres (133.20mph), fifty-miles (133.39mph), 100-kilometres (133.68mph), 200-miles (126.46mph), and 500-kilometres (120.18mph).

A small Renault, shared by Landon, Vernet, Pairaid and Fretet, broke eight Class H long distance records from 500-kilometres to twelve-hours at speeds of over 103mph, except for the 500 miles when the average fell to 102.79mph. A 492cc, flat-twin DB — driven by its designer, Robert Bonnet — ran for three hours at 99.10mph, collecting eight Class I records on the way, starting with fifty-miles at 101.35mph.

The Paris Grand Prix returned to Montlhéry in 1952 and proved a Ferrari 'benefit'. It lasted three hours and was won by Taruffi, who averaged 95.25mph for 285.85 miles in a 2-litre machine, in which he also set the fastest lap at 99.48mph. Simon's Ferrari, which covered 273.43 miles, was second, Farina's Ferrari taking third place ahead of Rosier (Ferrari), Lance Macklin (HWM), and Robert Manzon (Gordini).

Activity, other than the routine round of testing French products, did not commence at Montlhéry in 1953 until comparatively late in the year. However, in May, Rootes' new Sunbeam Alpine, the 2.2-litre, four-cylinder sporting car developed from the Sunbeam-Talbot 90 (not to be confused with the current Sunbeam Alpine which derives from the Rapier!) was demonstrated on the Belgian motorway, on which natlonal records were set. This car was then driven to Montlhéry and, with screen removed, the passenger seat faired over and an undershield attached; Leslie Johnson made the customary one hour run in it, averaging 110.56mph from a standing start and 111.20mph from a flying start. Then Stirling Moss had a go, lapping at over 115mph: indeed, his best lap was timed at 115.85mph.

After this, routine test work was resumed, if indeed it was ever interrupted. I remember dropping in on the Monday afternoon following the 1953 Le Mans race and finding plenty happening at the Paris track. Monotonously circulating were a Norton motorcycle, a Monneret motorcycle, and a Renault Frégate saloon. Renault was obviously finding Montlhéry useful, if a 4CV saloon towing a heavily-laden Renault van round and round was anything to judge by. Shorter runs were made by a Simca wearing a curious wooden body; an amateur-constructed, single-seater BMW (which, afterwards, refused to re-start), and a sports-racing Dyna-Panhard. At this time a special Salmson, with the then-new Solex double-choke carburetter, several more Renault Frégates, an Austin A40 laden with sandbags and doing petrol consumption checks (an indication, perhaps, of Alan Hess' desire to drive one of these cars from the Equator to the Arctic), and a Ford Vedette powered with a Citroën Light Fifteen engine, all came to Montlhéry for test work.

Late in September, Vinatier senior, Vinatier junior, and Barbot took out a Citroën 2CV with streamlined body and engine reduced in size, and broke international Class J records for 200-miles (57.19mph); 500-kilometres (57.30mph); 500-miles (57.40mph); 1000-kilometres (56.70mph); 1000-miles (54.20mph); 2000-kilometres (52.78mph); six-hours (57.50mph); twelve-hours (56.50mph), and twenty-four-hours (52.79mph).

In October John Cooper made successful attempts on shorter records in Class I (500cc) using a Cooper MkVII with a streamlined body in which the intrepid driver lay in a reclining position, covered by a perspex 'bubble'. The back wheels were enclosed and discs were used on the front wheels.

The engine was a 499cc Manx Norton belonging to tuning-wizard Francis Beart, running on Shell alcohol 60 fuel and Shell X100 SAE 60 lubricating oil. The attempt was not at all pleasant for poor John, for the nose-tank split and he spent most of the run soaked up to the waist in alcohol fuel, which – apart from the fumes – is highly inflammable, and stings and freezes the skin. However, he stuck to it bravely and the Cooper lapped at over 112mph, taking the fifty-kilometre record at 111.14mph; the fifty-miles at 111.30mph; the 100-kilometres at 111.4,0mph; the 100-miles at 112.35mph, and the 200-kilometres at 112.89mph. It then came in for an unscheduled depôt stop, because of the loss of fuel, and the tank was topped up. The Cooper carried on to take the hour record at 115.61mph, and the fastest lap was recorded at a speed of 116.33mph.

The following day Jack Fairman and Lance Macklin took out one of the Bristol Type 450 2-litre sports coupés which had been built for the Le Mans race, and broke six Class E records, covering 200-miles at 125.87mph; 500-kilometres at 116.10mph; 500-miles at 115.74mph; 1000-kilometres at 115.49mph, and taking, in additlon, the three-hour record at 116.42mph, and the six-hour record at 115.43mph. The car – the one Macklin had driven at Le Mans but now rather better streamlined – took a frightful battering on the rough Montlhéry bankings whilst lapping at nearly 130mph.

The engine finished in splendidly clean condition after having been held at 5700rpm for an hour and a half; it was using Shell fuel of ordinary pump quality. The engine was sealed and the car put away for the night. The next day Macklin and Fairman completed the run, after a morning spent in practice pit-stops. The only anxiety was breakage of the catches on the rear-hinged bonnet, which, fortunately, were also secured by straps. Only the rear Dunlop tyres required changing, and it is interesting that Selby used a very ingenious tool with which to cope with the G-type ERA wheels. These were attached by five nuts each. A tubular spanner contained each nut in its stem as it was removed, and these nuts were held there by a clamp until required, when, under the action of a spring, they returned down the stem one at a time, to be screwed home on the studs.

After the run was over Macklin took each mechanic round for a flying lap to show them the buffeting their work had so well stood up to, and to remind them that, at this speed round Montlhéry, a driver works hard, too! The Bristol was found to be capable of lapping as fast then as it had done before the run commenced; that is, at 126.11mph.

Meanwhile, Cooper had put a 350cc Manx Norton engine in his little streamlined car, and proceeded to break Class J records for fifty-kilometres (105.71mph); fifty-miles (104.93mph); 100-kilometres (105.10mph); 100-miles (104.39mph); 200-kilometres (103.87mph); 200-miles (103.46mph), and the hour (104.32mph). So well did the car run that the French officials measured the engine, only to find all correct, their calculations working out to 348cc. The little car ran faultlessly, lapping at nearly 110mph. Again John Cooper drove the car, lying down so low in the cockpit that he blistered the base of his spine on a cross-member; but, as he said, this position brought his crash helmet below the head cowling and was worth an extra 200rpm! The Cooper *équipe* was certainly making the most of its visit.

Francis Beart had installed a 596cc engine to enable the Cooper to run in Class H, but Eric Brandon tested this and was not satisfied, so the 500cc unit was converted to 530cc by substituting an 82mm barrel and piston. John Cooper drove the car non-stop in this form, breaking the Class H 200-kilometre record at 114.08mph. Hearing that Taruffi had booked Montlhéry for record work with his famous Gilera-engined Tarf, Cooper then re-installed the 500cc engine and improved his Class I figures by some 4mph on those established earlier in the week, to the speeds quoted above. However, these did not survive Taruffi's onslaught, the Italian raising the fifty-kilometre Class I record to 114.84mph; the fifty-miles to 115.94mph; the 100-kilometres to 114.10mph; the 100-miles to 114.80mph; the 200-kilometres to 115.39mph, and the hour record to 115.10mph.

Even these achievements were shortlived as J K Brise arrived later in October with a streamlined Arnott-Norton 500 and averaged 117.17mph for fifty-kilometres; 118.03mph for fifty-miles; 118.07mph for 100-kilometres; 118.02mph for 100-miles; 117.67mph for 200-kilometres; 115.53mph for 200-miles; 108.13mph for 500-kilometres, 117.76mph for one-hour, and 107.91mph for three-hours, with fastest lap timed at no less than 122mph.

Class H records for 100-kilometres (117.80mph); 100-miles (118.40mph), 200-kilometres (118.55mph), and the hour (118.57mph) were established, also in October, by a DB Panhard, which returned to average 114.20mph for 200-miles; 110.79mph for

500-kilometres, and 110.77mph for three-hours. The same make also broke Class G (1100cc) records for 200-miles (114.89mph); 500-kilometres (117.78mph); 500-miles (105.92mph); 1000-kilometres (106.92mph); three-hours (111.45mph), and six-hours (107.14mph).

Montlhéry had certainly seen a revival in record work during the 1953 season, as earlier in the year a whole series of Class E oil-engine records — from fifty-kilometres at 84.3mph to forty-eight hours at 76.76mph — had been established by a 1758cc, diesel-engined Borgward driven by Schaufele, Brudes, Nathan, Hartmann, Poch and Mouche, who distinguished themselves by setting up a total of fourteen Class E records, those for the full forty-eight-hours and for 5000-kilometres (81.22mph) being outright oil-engine Class records, irrespective of engine size.

During 1953 there also took place at Montlhéry a run of a different sort, which was quite unique. T H Plowman — a staunch 30/98 Vauxhall owner — was curious to discover how his 1924 version of this famous car would manage an hour's run on a banked track, and how he, at the age of 55, would cope with a high-speed drive of this nature. He had bought the Vauxhall, OE87, in 1934; engine OE200 had been installed after the original power unit had blown up at Brooklands in 1937. It was virtually a standard model, with racing 6.00 x 19 Dunlop tyres on the front wheels and 7.00 x 19S on the back wheels. It pulled an axle ratio of 13:40, had a compression-ratio of around 7:1, and ran on pump Esso petrol and Essolube oil. The non-original items were confined to larger inlet valves, a Tecalemit oil cooler and large capacity oil pump, a four-branch exhaust manifold and a single SU 1⅞ downdraught carburetter, a Hardy-Spicer propeller shaft, G-type brakes, and a front axle beam that lowered the chassis. The balanced crankshaft was used. The two-seater body had a fairing over the passenger seat, a radiator cowl, a dumb-iron apron, and a full-length undertray which left the sump exposed.

Plowman drove to Montlhéry and put in about seventeen training laps, during which he found the bankings very rough.

The special-bodied Bristol Type 450 coupé which took Class E records in 1953. (Bristol Aeroplane Co)

The old car received a fearful hammering, and he could hardly hold the steering wheel. He pulled up the front Hartford shock absorbers solid and enriched the mixture in the carburetter, then drove into Arpajon to buy a pair of chamois gloves to help him grip the wheel.

He returned to Montlhéry, the day being 6 August. M Massonet of the ACF was on hand to time the run officially in the late afternoon. A Simca was engaged in its pursuit of endurance records, but Plowman was told he could run providing he was forty per cent faster. He soon had the Vatuxhall above the yellow line, lapping in fifty-three seconds, so the officials were satisfied.

Lodge HLIP plugs were put in, the tank filled to the brim with twelve gallons of Esso, and the sump slightly (but deliberately) overfilled with oil. Soon the Vauxhall was being driven at full throttle, holding about 3400rpm, although along the brief straights the revs increased to some 3800rpm, equal to a speed of about 120mph. The best lap was at 109mph.

All the way round the front axle bottomed over the bumps, yet the anclent 30/98 didn't falter, and Plowman achieved his personal ambition of accomplishing over 100 miles in the hour with one of these fine cars. Indeed, the official distance was 106.9 miles, the run being timed from a flying start. The engine must have been developing about 130bhp, and fuel was consumed at the rate of about 12mpg.

After this magnificent achievement Plowman drove the car home to Luton via Dunkirk. He had given Bentley owners much to think about and, as will be seen in the next chapter, they were to spend much time, trouble and money before putting up anything like a comparable performance.

Chapter 17

1954 to the closure of Montlhéry

The 1954 season, so far as racing was concerned, began at Montlhéry on 25 April when two main races, the Coupe de Printemps and the Coupe de Paris, were contested, both over part of the combined track and road course. Both races were for touring and sports cars; the first confined to cars of up to 2-litres, over seventy-five kilometres, the latter for cars of 2-4½-litres over a distance of 100 kilometres.

English sportsmen were seen at these club-like races. In 1954 R Clarkson entered his Morgan Plus Four coupé with Triumph TR engine, which put it in the under-2-litres category; A P Hitchings drove a Ford-powered Lotus, and J Horridge a home-built special with a Riley Sprite engine in a Jowett Jupiter chassis.

First day of practice was marred by a fatal accident that befell Guy Mairesse, who was baulked at the junction of the road and track sections of the course — after coming down the straight at 140mph — by a 4CV Renault which had got lost and was dithering in the middle of the course. He spun his Talbot through a concrete barrier, killing himself and three child spectators in the process.

G Olivier drove an open Porsche in the Coupe de Printemps. This was the car that had been exhibited at the 1953 Paris Salon, but with its four-camshaft engine exchanged for a normal '1500' push-rod power unit. This Porsche proved unbeatable and Olivier drove with notable verve to win in 34min 50sec at an average speed of 129.127mph. He was followed home by M Balsa's 328 BMW-engined Veritas coupé and A Martignoni's 1900 Alfa-Romeo TT saloon.

These three cars were soon out on their own, but Clarkson kept up with them for a few laps, until the Morgan burnt a hole in a piston. The Lotus suffered from a broken crankshaft and the Riley Special from damage to its pre-selector gearbox.

The field which lined up for the Coupe de Paris race was even more varied, for a normal Citroën Six saloon came out in company with an Arnott 500 and an ex-works C-type Jaguar. J Duncan Hamilton won in his disc-braked XK120C Jaguar, which had been the factory's spare car during 1953. The only preparation the Jaguar (which had been driven to Montlhéry from Dieppe) required was the fitting of 'hard' plugs; it held 135-140mph on the banking, rising to 155mph on the straight.

Hamilton averaged 93.84mph, covering the 100-kilometres in 40min 10.2sec, which left the second car home, da Silva Ramos' 2.9-litre Aston Martin — a DB2 with DB3 engine using Weber carburetters — a lap behind. J Thepenier finished third at the wheel of an early 1½-litre Gordini.

The race was a rather dull procession, but Keeling managed to end up in the ditch, unhurt, as his XK120C Jaguar was lapping a slower competitor, and when he was second behind Duncan Hamilton. Actually, the entry was divided into classes, but with a small field this meant that some classes consisted of a lone entry, whilst the 1½-litre Porsche that had won the Coupe de Printemps was permitted to race again, as in this event racing cars of 750cc to 4½-litres joined the sports and touring cars.

The day's sport concluded with two heats and a final for some thirty French drivers in the new Monomill single-seaters which René Bonnet had contrived from 850cc DB components. For this a special shortened course sufficed.

The Bol d'Or endurance race of twenty-four hours' duration returned to Montlhéry on 29-30 May. Formerly this had really been an endurance test, because only one driver was permitted per car. Often the same luckless man would ride in the twenty-four hour motorcycle race and, after very little rest, come out again for another twenty-four hour drive in a car. However, for 1954 the rules were altered to permit two drivers to share a car, while capacity limit was now 1600cc.

Thirty-eight entries were received, and the course used was the 6.3 kilometre combined track and road circuit. At 5.45pm the drivers got away to a Le Mans start, but the two English entrants, John Horridge with the aforementioned Horridge Special, and R Hardy with his Lotus, were still filling their fuel tanks. They excused themselves with the remark that, as for once the start of the free-and-easy Bol d'Or was only half an hour late, this had caught them unawares, but when they were ready they joined in.

After an hour Olivier's very fast Porsche – which he was sharing with the now-famous French woman driver Gilberte Thirion – was leading, followed by the de Burney/Etienne DB Panhard and an all-enveloping Fiat 1500 Special with triple Solex carburetters. Behind this came another special, in the form of the Ferry-Renault 4CV, with its engine at the front of a tubular chassis and a normal, non-independent back axle – all of which was in the best Bol d'Or tradition! When darkness came the spectators saw single-seater racing cars running with lamps ablaze, another Bol d'Or peculiarity, for there was a class for racing cars up to 1100cc.

Pit-work was carefree and comic. Poor Mlle Thirion drove on and on without seeing any signals from the badly-equipped Porsche pit, whereas the English entrants had agreed to work as a team, and good neon-tube signals were displayed from their pit. The Bol d'Or was again living up to tradition in the matter of mechanical troubles ingeniously repaired. A Peugeot 203 ran a big-end, so its driver set about dismantling the engine and replacing it. Gerry Crombac, sharing the Lotus with Hardy, ran into the ditch and damaged the car's front suspension, so he drove to Paris for some spares he had, returned to Montlhéry, and let Hardy carry these to the stricken car. Repairs were carried out at the roadside, and the Lotus was back in the race after four hours.

As the long race ran on, now in hot sunshine, the Porsche retired with broken crown wheel and pinion, the Fiat 1500 Special ran a big-end, and the little Ferry-Renault took the lead from an MD-Peugeot coupé. When the Ferry-Renault came in for re-fuelling it refused to re-start. The rules said engines must be started on the self-starter so, when a change of battery brought no response, the team concluded that the starter motor had burnt out. Again Bol d'Or tradition prevailed, for Eugène Mauve, the power behind all these races, agreed to a push-start provided the car did not get pushed beyond the pit area. This worked, and it resumed the race, but amid much discussion, in which some people reluctantly talked of protesting. However, the little car resolved a difficult situation by retiring soon afterward with an ominous clonk and the appearance of a pool of lubricant under its crankcase.

With one hour's racing left, twenty-one cars were still competing, albeit some very slowly. The Fiat 1500 was doing a lap every so often; the Lotus required a great deal of water because the head gasket was blowing, and a 4CV Renault was circulating slowly with loudly protesting big-ends. The MD-Peugeot still led but, with only minutes to go, it fell sick, running more and more slowly, so that this admirable race became exciting. It looked as if the Horridge Special might win after all. This it just failed to do, the result being:

1st	J Sigrand/Celerier (MD-Peugeot)	2554.417km, 66.5mph
2nd	J Horridge/G Trouis (Horridge-Riley)	2506.896km
3rd	J Prieur/A Prieur (Simca Special)	2432.143km
4th	de Voos/Baldini (Simca-Cesure)	2418.430km
5th	Biasuz/Atienza (Simca Junior)	2373.689km
6th	J George/Costa (Panhard)	2348.292km

Racing had certainly got into its stride at Montlhéry in 1954, for on 10 October a race meeting was put on to coincide with the Paris Salon motor exhibition. As usual, the main event was the Coupe du Salon. The course used was the 6.3 kilometres in which the cars negotiated the northern banking in the reverse direction from that used for normal outer circuit racing, and took in part of the road circuit.

A small but select field of twenty-nine very fast sports cars contested the Coupe du Salon, which was a scratch contest over twenty-four laps, divided into 750cc, 1500cc, 2000cc and unlimited categories. Fastest practice lap was achieved by Jean Behra, driving the works 3-litre Le Mans Gordini with central driving seat. He was to compete against Masten Gregory's 4½-litre Ferrari, Grignard's works supercharged 2.8-litre Pegaso two-seater (which had right-hand steering and many cooling louvres), Levegh's Talbot, Duncan Hamilton's XK120C disc-braked Jaguar, Picard's 750S Monza Ferrari, da Silva Ramos' works 2-litre, six-cylinder Gordini, five 2-litre Maseratis, the 1½-litre Connaughts of Kenneth MacAlpine and Stirling Moss, a Lotus, some OSCAs, a Porsche 550, a supercharged Peugeot Special, and the inevitable Lago-Talbots.

Quickly Jean Behra established his supremacy, drawing away in the lead with Duncan Hamilton holding off Masten Gregory's Ferrari for second place, until the latter went past the Jaguar, Hamilton then battling with Picard's Ferrari and Levegh's Talbot. Moss led the 1½-litre class comfortably, ahead of Veuillet's Porsche. Pegaso, that exotic Spanish make, was represented by an unsupercharged 3.2-litre car driven by the works driver Palacio, as well as by Grignard's blown 2.8, but neither ran at all well.

The two leaders, Behra and Gregory, were running unchallenged but were nevertheless driving close to the limit. Now Peron speeded up his Tour de France OSCA with new eight-plug head and led the Porsche and Connaught in the 1½-litre class. The 2-litre category looked like a victory for da Silva Ramos' Gordini, but a rocker broke and he had to retire with only four laps to go.

That left the Maseratis dominating the class. In the smallest category a fine duel was being fought between Orsetti's Giannini-engined Giaur and the Ferry-Renault which had nearly won the Bol d'Or. Moss eventually found Peron slowing and managed to win the 1½-litre class.

Behra won under a wintry sky, setting a new car lap record for the course in 2min 16sec (103.95mph). The final result was:

1st   J Behra (Gordini) 55min 56.2sec, 101.1mph

2nd	M Gregory (Ferrari) 55min 41.4sec
3rd	J D Hamilton (Jaguar) 57min 57.2sec
4th	F Picard (Ferrari) 57min 58.0sec
5th	P Levegh (Talbot) 58min 9.0sec

No other competitors completed the full distance

Class winners

750cc	C Orsetti (Giaur) 19laps in 58min 19.0sec
1500cc	S Moss (Connaught) 22 laps in 57min 2.6sec
2000cc	B Musy (Maserati) 23 laps in 57min 17 sec

Unlimited: J Behra (Gordini) 24 laps in 55min 56.2sec

That morning, before the Coupe du Salon, a race for tuned production cars had been held over seventeen laps of the same course, which the R K N Clarkson TR-engined Morgan Plus Four coupé led from start to fnish. It won in 51min 36sec at 77.1mph from P Chavy's supercharged Peugeot 203 saloon and Mme Ferray's Porsche 1500. Another contest in the Monomill Circus was also staged.

Record breaking in 1954 was confined to October, when Pierro Taruffi used his twin-boom Gilera twin-cylinder Tarf Italcorsa to break the Class I (500cc) fifty-kilometre record at 124.92mph; the fifty-mile record at 125.62mph, and the 100-mile record at 121.59mph. About a week later the same driver and car were out again, and this time the Class I 100-kilometre record fell at 124.21mph; the 100-mile record at 124.73mph; the 200-kilometre record at 124.76mph, and the one-hour record at 124.77mph. On 17 October, between these Italian attempts, Robert Bonnet appeared with his DB Panhard and lifted the Class H (750cc) fifty-mile record to 121.67mph; the 100-kilometre record to 121.94mph; the 100-mile record to 122.53mph; the 200-kilometre record to 122.64mph, and the one-hour record to 122.61mph.

Finally, on 10 December P Chancel came out with a 610cc, two-cylinder, air-cooled, Dyna-Panhard claimed to develop 85bhp, and turn at 5700rpm. Chancel succeeded in breaking Bonnet's records by a comfortable margin, averaging speeds of 124.41mph for fifty-kilometres; 124.98mph for fifty-miles; 125.21mph for 100-kilometres; 125.53mph for 100-miles; 125.47mph for 200-kilometres, and 125.45mph for the hour: no mean speeds for a tiny car running in Class H. It had an all-enveloping body and ran at the very top of the bankings.

The 1955 Montlhéry season began on 7 April with the Coupe de Paris race, which was open to cars of all kinds but which was regarded generally as a sports car contest. Run over sixteen laps, or about 101 kilometres, of the 6.3-kilometre circuit, it resulted in bad feeling because, although Duncan Hamilton from England had made fastest practice time with his C-type Jaguar, the Belgian driver André Pilette, driving for the Gordini factory, was allowed to substitute a 2½-litre Grand Prix Gordini for the 3-litre eight-cylinder sports Gordini in which he had practised. The reason given was that the sports car had developed trouble at the end of the practice session, too late for repairs to be effected. Not only that, but Pilette was permitted to line up his 'racer' on the front row of the starting grid alongside Hamilton and the Marquis de Portago – who had earned their front-row places on practice times – the latter driving Rosier's old 4½-litre Ferrari which had been converted into a sports car.

Naturally, the Gordini won, at 101.13mph, by a considerable margin. Duncan Hamilton's Jaguar finished second, F Picard's 750S Ferrari third, and de Portago fourth. Hamilton had, in any case, had a horrid drive, because the shock absorbers of his Jaguar were damaged when it skidded on a patch of wet tar early in the race and hit the roadside bank, its handling on the banking thereafter being decidedly precarious.

On 14-15 May the Bol d'Or twenty-four hour sports car race was again staged at Montlhéry. The general category was a victory for Veuillet and Olivier driving a Porsche Spyder, in which they completed a distance of 1974 miles at an average speed of 82.22mph. Second place was taken by Jeser and Mme Bousquet wlth another Porsche, which covered 1941 miles, while the

The Austin-Healey of the BMC high-speed, long distance team passes the grandstand in 1955. (A G Goodchild)

Guyot/Parsy Maserati was placed third, having done 1902 miles. These three cars were some 150 miles ahead of the next to finish: Ramos and Pollet in a Gordini; de Cortanze and Dernier in a Peugeot, and Barbier and Chambas, also driving a Peugeot. Class winners were the Stempert/Bonnet DB in the 750cc category, the winning Porsche in the 1½-litre class, and the Maserati in the 2-litre category.

Nineteen-fifty-five saw some more one hour demonstration runs at the Paris track, the most ambitious being by the British Motor Corporation, which took over a Riley Pathfinder saloon, an Austin Healey 100, an MGA, a Wolseley 6/90 saloon, and an Austin A90 Westminster saloon. The team of drivers appointed for these cars were, respectively, R C Porter, Ron Flockhart, Ken Wharton, and John Gott for the last three vehicles. In an hour they ran, respectively, 108.03, 104.32, 102.54, 112.36, 101.20 and 101.99 miles, so that the makers were able to advertise that each of these products could exceed 'the ton' for sustained periods, although the cars concerned were, in fact, tuned to FIA Group 3 and 4 standards.

Actual performances of these BMC products were as follows:

R C Porter (Riley Pathfinder)

50km	108.72mph
100km	108.09mph
1 hour	108.03mph
50 miles	108.17mph
100 miles	108.02mph

R Flockhart (Austin-Healey 100)

50km	104.55mph
100km	104.34mph
1 hour	104.32mph
50 miles	104.42mph
100 miles	104.30mph

J Gott (MGA Stage ll tune)
50km	112.99mph
100km	112.20mph
1 hour	112.36mph
50 miles	112.39mph
100 miles	112.23mph

J Gott (Austin A90 Westminster)
50km	101.51mph
100km	101.82mph
1 hour	101.99mph
50 miles	101.74mph
100 miles	101.98mph

K Wharton (MGA)
50km	102.64mph
100km	102.92mph
1 hour	102.54mph
50 miles	102.71mph
100 miles	102.52mph

J Gott (Wolseley 6/90)
50km	101.56mph
100km	101.22mph
1 hour	101.20mph
50 miles	101.35mph
100 miles	101.19mph

Attempts occurred on two different days. John Gott had two runs with the Austin, because a tyre burst during his first attempt.

The MGA in Serles II tune had a 3.7 top gear, an undertray, screen, bumpers and hood removed. It was cruised at 5700rpm, and fastest lap was approximately 114mph. Porter took three passengers in the Riley Pathfinder, cruised it at about 5300rpm and did a best lap of approximately 110mph. In the MGA Wharton ran with hood and side-screens erect, the engine turning over at 6000rpm. The cars were tuned in respect of non-standard compression-ratios (the Riley used a cr of 8.6:1, the Austin A90 a cr of 8:1) and special valve springs. The Austin had twin SU carburetters in place of the single Zenith carburetter fitted as standard, and, along with the Riley Pathfinder and the Wolseley 6/90, was given higher-than-standard back axle ratios (3.7:1). These runs certainly showed how very rapidly ordinary cars could be made to go by 1955, especially as they ran on pump petrol.

On 17 October the Cooper Car Company from Surbiton made a splendidly successful onslaught on Class G records, using a rear-engined Coventry-Climax-powered sports car.

The engine had a prototype high-lift-camshaft and developed 83bhp. The chassis tubes were of heavier gauge than normal, and heavier shock absorbers, an extra petrol pump, long-range tanks, and a special driving seat were used.

Charles and John Cooper supervised the attempt. Jim Russell, Arthur Owen and Bill Knight drove the car, the best lap at a speed of 132.56mph, a very fine performance for a single-cam car running on Esso pump fuel and standard Essolube oil. Freak gearing was not employed, or the standing-start lap – at no less than 101.79mph, a new track record – would not have been possible. Petrol consumption of about 35mpg was recorded. Incidentally, even the drivers' Timex watches were British.

Broken Class G records were as follows: fifty-kilometres (128.27mph); fifty-miles (127.73mph); 100-kilometres (127.36mph); 100-miles (125.86mph); 200-kilometres (125.37mph); one-hour (125.34mph); 200-miles (118 .35mph); 500-kilometres (115.30mph); three-hours (115.26mph); 500-miles (112.88mph); 1000-kilometres (111,55mph); six-hours (111.63mph).

There is an excellent account of this and other Cooper record attempts at Montlhéry in *The Racing Coopers* by Arthur Owen (Cassell, 1959).

Montlhéry enjoyed a face-lift before the 1956 season when the road circuit was re-surfaced and the corner near the banked track provided with a four-foot high concrete safety wall with earth embankment beyond it to give spectators a good vantage point. Entirely new ferro-concrete pits were constructed with pressure re-fuelling equipment for each, and a balcony above.

The Bol d'Or was replaced by a 1000-kilometre sports car race, the first major race to be held in France after the terrible Le Mans disaster of 1955. The starting area was divided by a line of straw bales to form a proper 'road' of the banking and out to the road circuit; the remaining wide area became a bypass pull-in to the pits. A white line before the end of the banking indicated entry into the pits bypass; when a car was seen to be coming in, the gendarmes sounded a shrill warning on their whistles. From the pits a very narrow straw bale 'lane' led back to the course.

For the 1000-kilometre race a 7.784 kilometre circuit was employed which took in the eastern banking and turned back at the sharp bends at La Côte Lapize.

An excellent entry of thirty cars was received and competitors were given three separate practice periods; the Thursday and Friday evenings preceding the start, and another on the Saturday morning, with the race starting at 10.30am on the Sunday.

The course chosen proved very hard on men and machines, and poor weather conditions did not help, but it was a fast circuit, Jean Behra lapping at nearly 100mph in practice.

Factory entries were confined to the Behra/Rosier 3-litre Maserati, two 1½-litre AWEs, and two works supported Ecurie Monopole Panhards. Otherwise, this was a race of amateurs, with a field of great variety – Monza Ferrari, Mondial Ferrari, Porsche Spyder, 200S Maserati, a DB3S Aston Martin for Ken Wharton, A6G Maseratis, twin-cam Gordini, 150S Maseratis, DB Panhard, Ferry-Renault, VP Renault, Stanguellini and Moretti.

There were four classes for 750cc, 1½-litre, 2-litre and 3-litre cars, and the course had to be covered 129 times. Each driver had to do a minimum of thirty laps but not more than fifty without refuelling.

In a fine Grand Prix-type start Trintignant's Monza Ferrari took the lead, but soon it was Behra's red 300S Maserati which headed the pack, the faster cars passing the pits at nearly 140mph. In the 2-litre category the Gordini of da Silva Ramos was going splendidly, though strongly pursued by the two AWEs. The new four-cylinder, twin-overhead camshaft Gordini was leading the 1½-litre class, and the Monopole-Panhards, as befitted 'works' cars, led the small fry.

After an hour Behra led Trintignant, who was hampered by a broken windscreen, Schell's Monza Ferrari was third, and de Portago's Monza Ferrari fourth, very close up.

Manzon's Gordini was not handling at all well round the banking. Wharton's Aston Martin was duelling with an AWE, and female driver, Gilberte Thirion, was second in her Mondial Ferrari in the 2-litre class.

At the first thirty lap pit-stops confusion reigned for a time because someone had forgotten to turn on the main fuel supply and pit staff found their hoses dry. Wharton wisely sent Kyffin off without fuel, but Rosenhammer left in a fury and ditched his 1½-litre AWE irrevocably. Munaron overturned his 3-litre Gordini just before he was due in, luckily without personal injury.

Schell got past Trintignant and later led the race as Rosier took over from Behra – the Maserati pit this time having ready churns of fuel in case the hoses again played up. Rosier was soon back in the lead and maintaining the pace. When the heavy rain eventually stopped speeds increased, Phil Hill going round notably quickly in the Monza Ferrari he shared with de Portago. When the tank sprang a bad leak, the latter's legs were soaked in fuel.

The Aston Martin had retired with gearbox failure, many other cars had fallen out, and, in the 2-litre class it was now the two women drivers, Thirion and de Filippis, who fought for the lead.

In spite of having a comfortable lead, Behra drove at lap record speed, and, on his last lap, averaged 103.03mph, another fastest time. The Maserati ran out of fuel on its lap of honour, because a leak had developed in the tank. The course was closed an hour later, four 750cc cars having to be flagged off. The results were:

1st	Behra/Rosier (Maserati) 6hr 41min 3.1sec, 97.025mph	
2nd	Schell/Lucas (Ferrari) 6hr 43min 44.3sec	
3rd	Trintignant/Picard (Ferrari) 6hr 44min 22.3sec	
4th	Pilette/Milhoux (Ferrari) 6hr 53min 51.8sec	
5th	de Portago/Hill (Ferrari) 6hr 58min 37.6sec	
6th	Landi/Gerini (Maserati) 7hr 16min 3 .6sec	

Fastest lap
Behra 2min 50sec 103.03mph

Class winners
750cc   Laureau/Hechard (DB Panhard)
1500cc   Goethals/Harris (Porsche)
3000cc   Mlle Thirion/Mlle Peduzzi (Ferrari)

The other Montlhéry race of the 1956 season was the traditional Coupe du Salon, held on 7 October over a distance of 150 kilometres on the combined road and track circuit. It was a very sad occasion, because Benoit Musy went over the banking when the steering of his 2-litre Maserati failed, and veteran Louis Rosier crashed in his Monza Ferrari; both accidents ultimately proved fatal, although poor Rosier lingered for three weeks.

The race was won by F Godia's 300S Maserati in 1hr, 0min, 54.7sec at a speed of 92.22mph from J Duncan Hamilton's D-type Jaguar (a regular British entrant at these French races) (1hr 1min 30.7sec , and third place was taken by Jean Behra's 2½-litre Lago-Talbot (1hr 1min 47.2 sec). Goethal's Porsche, Loens' Maserati, Piper's Lotus and Blanche's Ferry-Renault won their respective classes, and de Portago's 3-litre Ferrari Europa won the Grand Touring and Modifed Touring Car Race at 87.42mph from Peron's Ferrari Europa and Houel's 300SL Mercédès-Benz. In this race the up-to-1300cc class was dominated by three Alfa-Romeo Giuliettas, driven by Loyer, Nicol and Dutoit, the winner averaging

81.84mph. In the main race Musy set fastest lap at 93.31mph, before his unhappy accident. Record attempts were confined to Utah and Monza, Montlhéry being singularly peaceful in 1956.

Record breaking returned to the Paris track in 1957, although all the faster International Class and world records attempts now occurred at Monza or Utah. However, at Montlhéry a Simca Aronde saloon successfully broke long duration records in Class F (1100-1500cc). It ran for a total of thirty-eight days, capturing, on the way, the twenty-nine-day record at 70.41mph, the 50,000-miles at 70.27mph, the thirty-days at 70.28mph, the thirty-one-days at 70.28mph, the thirty-two-days at 70.30mph, the thirty-three-days at 70.18mph, the 90,000-kilometres at 70.19mph, the thirty-four-days at 70.22mph, the 60,000-miles at 70.25mph, the thirty-five days at 70.23mph, the thirty-six days at 70.25mph, 100,000-kilometres at 70.24mph, the thirty-seven-days at 70.23mph and the thirty-eight-day record at 70.06mph. Thls was a splendid achievement for a small family saloon, and Simca thus assumed the mantle previously worn by Citroën. Simca has continued to make long duration runs of this kind, the latest being an unofficial duration record at the disused, unbanked Miramas track. I was at Montlhéry just before the 1957 records were established, being driven there by one of the test staff, and was able to drive a few rapid laps in a similar Simca Elysée saloon. The team which drove the record-breaking car were: M Ganthier, R Duhan, R Pavy, F Targiani, J Calleja, L Broquet, N Benoit, Y Hamond and R Madiesse.

Some more long duration records were established by a team of young Cambridge undergraduates. Using an Austin A35 saloon, and assisted by Marcus Chambers, manager of the British Motor Corporation (who also drove), they set seven Class G records, averaging 74.79mph for 10,000-miles; 74.83mph for 15,000-kilometres; 74.89mph for 20,000-kilometres; 74.91mph for four-days; 74.96mph for five-days; 74.83mph for six-days, and 74.90mph for seven-days: a very consistent week's motoring. The team, apart from Chambers, comprised R Simpson, P Rivière,

T Threlfall, A Taylor and G Horrocks. The little Austin was virtually standard, except for a long-range fuel tank, higher axle ratio, a 30mm instead of 60mm carburetter, an oil-cooler, and some additional instruments. In the seven days and nights it covered a total of 12,580 miles.

In Class K a 250cc Isetta-Velam, driven by C Peslier and J Bianchi, set Class K records for 1000-kilometres (68.28mph); 1000-miles (67.95mph); 2000-kilometres (68.02mph); twelve- hours (68.10mph), and twenty-four-hours (68.10mph): pretty good for such a diminutive motor car for such a long time. Later, the Isetta set the Class K 200-kilometre record to 67.81mph and the three-hour record to 69.50mph.

Racing at Montlhéry during 1957 embraced the Prix de Paris, which was run over 151 kilometres, or twenty-four laps of the 6.3-kilometre road-and-track circuit. Competitors were a mixture of Formula 2 racing cars, sports cars, and Gran Turismo cars, so that British F2 Coopers were able to dominate the field. Jack Brabham won in 1hr 2min 45.7sec, at a speed of 90.2mph, from M McDowell, A Marsh and Ivor Bueb, all in Coopers, Brabham making fastest lap at 92.72mph on his third circuit.

Of the sports car races, the Coupe de Vitesse was run in April, over seventy kilometres, and was won by de Portago's Ferrari at an average speed of 138.37mph from Cornet's Maserati and Piper's Lotus. In September the thirty-lap Coupe d'Automne race saw Hicks' Lotus victorious, at 91.91mph, from Le Guezai's Mercédès-Benz and Chardonnat's AC Bristol.

There was not a great deal of activity at Montlhéry in 1958 that was of importance outside local testing and experimental runs. In June the Grand Prix de Paris meeting was repeated, the main race being for Formula 2 racing cars over the usual road-cum-track course. Of 100 kilometres, it was a Cooper-Climax 'benefit' with these cars occupying the first five places.

The winner was Henry Taylor in a time of 39min 46.8sec and average speed of 94.87mph. He was followed home by A Guelfi, B McLaren, I Burgess, and A Marsh, in that order.

Then, at Paris Salon time, the Coupe du Salon meeting took place as usual, but unhappily under wet weather conditions. It was not a very inspiring spectacle, for a contest between a team of Italian Formula Junior cars and the Panhard-powered Monomills was termed a Franco-Italian duel, but was won by the Portuguese driver of a Stanguellini!

The Gran Turismo race over a mere twelve laps, or 75½ kilometres, was won by Bianchi's Ferrari 250GT in 33min 57.0sec, at a speed of 83.39mph, from similar Ferraris driven by J P Schild and C Bourillot. R Hicks finished fourth in his Lotus Eleven, a curious GT car, ahead of Jean Behra's Porsche Carrera and P Berney's Alfa-Romeo Giulietta Zagato. Bianchi established fastest lap at 85.17mph.

The Formula 2 race, over twenty laps, or 125.8 kilometres, was better stuff, although, in the end, this, too, developed into a dull procession, Jim Russell leading Jack Brabham home, with N Barclay third and Keith Ballisat fourth, all driving twin-cam Cooper-Climax cars. Parkes' Fry-Climax had retired on the first lap, Bueb's Lotus was outclassed by the Coopers, Vidille's Cooper left the road, and Marsh's Cooper retired. Russell won in 53min 29.9sec, at 88.2mph, after making fastest lap at 90.04mph.

A 2-litre sports car race saw Tavano's Ferrari win at 85.77mph from Schiller's Porsche and Honel's Porsche, while later in 1958 Tavano (Ferrari) also won the Coupe d'Automne at 73.51mph from Hicks' Lotus Eleven and Perrier's OSCA.

International record breaking in 1958 was confined to an Austin-Healey which Taylor, Horrocks, Threlfall, Simpson, Jones, Clarke and Summers took to Montlhéry for the purpose of challenging Class D long distance records. They circulated for four days, in the course of which they took the 5000-mile record at 98.50mph; the 10,000-kilometre record at 97.31mph; the 10,000-mile record at 97.13mph; the 15,000-kilometre record at 97.04mph; the two-days at 98.73mph; the three-days at 98.73mph, and the four-day record at 97.04mph – very easy to record on paper, but, in fact, an undertaking calling for the careful preparation and attention to detail that every successful record attempt requires.

Knight and Owen also had a go at the recently-recognized Class K (up to 250cc) records with a Cooper, and took those for 200-kilometres (86.51mph); 200-miles (84.39mph); three-hours (76.51mph); 500-kilometres (78.22mph); six-hours (79.10mph), and 500-miles (79.44mph).

Even less of international importance occurred at Montlhéry in 1959. This year, for a change, the traditional Coupe du Salon meeting was held in scorching sunshine. The twenty-six lap, 163 kilometre Formula 2 race was contested entirely by Coopers, with the exception of Hicks' early F2 Lotus. Harry Schell won at 95.9mph, after a drive lasting 12hr 3min 57.4sec; J Lewis was second, J Campbell-Jones third, H Taylor fourth, and R Collomb a very slow fifth. Taylor had been hampered by gear lever trouble, Bianchi crashed the Equipe Belge Cooper, and Gibson suffered the indignity of a puncture. The lone Lotus succumbed to transmission trouble. Harry Schell lapped fastest, at 98.25mph, a new circuit lap record.

The GT race was also rather dull, because Bianchi was a non-starter in the Tour de France-winning Ferrari 250GT, which burnt a hole in a piston in practice, and gearbox trouble soon put Noblet's Ferrari out of the race, which was then a walkover for Schild, the Swiss driver of another Ferrari 250GT. Hicks, in his Lotus Eleven, duelled throughout the entire race with Lefebvre (Lotus Eleven) and won the 1300cc category, these drivers beating Persons' Porsche Carrera. But, again, how did Lotus Elevens qualify as GT cars?

Earlier in 1959 the Prix de Paris race, also a Formula 2 event, had been run over 157 kilometres, the winner being Lewis' Cooper-Climax, at 95.7mph, from Barclay's Cooper-Climax, with Schell's Porsche RSK taking third place. On the same day a sixty-seven kilometre race was run for Formula Junior cars, May's Stanguellini winning at 61mph from Alberti and Borden, also in Stanguellinis. The Gran Turismo race at this meeting was a victory for Gendebien's Ferrari 250GT, averaging 80.45mph for the 100-kilometres, second and third places going to Bourillot's and Seidel's sister cars.

A very interesting event took place at Montlhéry in May, when members of the Bentley Drivers' Club took their cars to the track to see how vintage vehicles could perform. As a matter of fact, the BDC had paid a disastrous visit to Monza the previous year, their various Bentleys failing to complete an hour's run at high speed. In 1959 they took seven vintage Bentleys to Antwerp and put up some extremely good times on the motor road. Forrest Lycett in his famous 8-litre achieved the fastest mean speed of 141.131mph for the flying start kilometre. After this McDonald and Stanley Sedgwick drove to Montlhéry, in their 4½- and 6½-litre vintage Bentleys. George McDonald lapped at 116.8mph, but after forty minutes of the intended hour a piston broke.

George Burton drove Sedgwick's stark 6½-litre Bentley, and got round at no less than 123.38mph, although a carburetter fire put paid to the run after forty-five minutes. In fact, the 4½-litre Bentley completed 71¼ miles at 110.98mph before retiring, and the 6½-litre Bentley over 88½ miles at 117.77mph. In spite of these fine speeds from old machinery, the BDC referred to its Montlhéry visit as 'unfinished business' and — perhaps with Plowman's hour run in 1953 in his 30/98 Vauxhall in mind — declared that it would return to Paris the following year to finish the job.

And return it did in 1960; this time G G McDonald achieved his ambition. Arriving in the course of a tour with his family in his well-known 4½-litre Bentley, he took it on to the track and, under official observation, covered 110.85 miles in the hour from a standing start, 111.18 miles from a flying start, and a best lap speed of 114.92mph.

Gerry Crozier also tried for the 'hour', in Sedgwick's Speed Six 6½-litre Bentley. After fifty miles he had averaged 121.15mph from a flying start, and 100 miles were covered at an average speed of 120.62mph before the engine gave trouble. G Burton's 4½-litre Bentley and D McKenzie's 3-litre Bentley also essayed the hour

*Willy Mairesse slides his Ferrari 250GT in the 1000
Kilometres de Paris of 1960. (Jacques L Chevry)*

run but both were forced to give up; Burton with a burnt piston
and McKenzie with lubrication trouble. The fine speeds achieved
by them both greatly impressed the French authorities, as did the
potential and fine state of preservation of the British vintage cars.
Moreover, a Bentley had at last, after many vicissitudes, beaten the
achievement of Plowman's lone 30/98 Vauxhall!

Racing commenced on 15 May with the thirty-lap Prix de Paris race for Formula 2 racing cars. Maurice Trintignant not only won, driving a Cooper-Climax, at 83.23mph, but also made fastest lap at 84.83mph. Second place went to J Lewis' Cooper-Climax; third place to J Twisk's TS-Climax. Cabral's Cooper-Climax was a lap behind, Goethal's Porsche RSK two laps behind, and Hicks' Lotus three laps in arrears.

In October the Coupe du Salon was held again, but only nine cars started in this sixteenth race of the series. Laureau crashed in his Cooper while practising, and Tim Parnell's and André Pilette's Reg Parnell Coopers were held up so long at the French frontier – after having been driven through the night from Innsbruck – that they did not arrive in time to start.

Again, pouring rain was the order of the day. Although not on the front row of the grid, Schlesser's Cooper led for two of the fifty laps of the 3.3-kilometre road and track circuit before being overtaken by Bianchi's Cooper-Climax; after eleven laps Lewis' Cooper-Climax went ahead. Lewis built up a useful lead in appalling weather conditions to win at 69.38mph (1hr 30min 14.4sec) for the 167 kilometres. Bianchi was second, less than a minute behind, and Utley was placed third in Hicks' 1959 Lotus-Climax. Schlesser retired with defective engine bearings. Turner, in the Emeryson-Climax, drove well to pass Utley after he had lost two laps due to spinning off, only to be disqualifed because he had failed on a number of laps to negotiate the straw bale chicane which had been built just before the banking. Lewis, in winning his second Formula 2 race at Montlhéry in two years, made fastest lap at 70.94mph.

In view of the excellence of the Montlhéry road-cum-banked circuit, it seems a great pity that more notable races have not been run there in recent years. The fact is that the small organization responsible for events such as the Coupe du Salon has insufficient capital to put on anything bigger, and outside this organization all of the money is spent on racing at Reims and Rouen. The circuit has, for the past two years, been put to good use by a Swiss school for training racing drivers, and, at the time of the Paris

Salon, the entire road circuit is given over on a Sunday to visiting foreign journalists who test French cars over it. But so good a circuit deserves better use, so I am delighted that the last race with which this book [the original edition] deals is the 1000 kilometre Gran Turismo race held at Montlhéry on 23 October 1960, which was an excellent and important event, with a fine field of thirty-four cars.

The course used was the 7.8-kilometre circuit, and again a chicane of straw bales was erected at the entry to the banked track. Even so, in practice Gendebien's Ferrari 250GT lapped in 2min 58.3sec. British hopes that the privately-entered 3.7-litre DB4GT Aston Martins of John Ogler would win were shattered, for the Innes Ireland/Roy Salvadori car could not better 3min 8.2sec, and the Clark/Maggs car 3min 10.3sec.

The usual damp, depressing weather prevailed at the track at the start, although a weak sun was attempting to dispel the mist that enshrouded Paris. From a 'Le Mans' start the many Ferraris streamed away from the Aston Martins.

The Crombac/Francis Abarth stopped almost immediately with ignition trouble, and the race soon became dominated by the impressive Ferrari 250GT cars, in the order of Gendebien, Mairesse, Schlesser, Scarlatti, Guichet, Loustel, with Ireland's Aston Martin seventh, and Clark's Aston Martin later coming up to eighth place. Graham Hill's 'works' Porsche was eleventh and leading the 1000-1600cc Class.

Interest was maintained only because the two Belgian drivers, Gendebien and Mairesse, were continually changing places for the lead, and as often setting new lap records. After going round at 93.1mph, Mairesse came into his pit to change a front wheel on lap nineteen, having damaged it by brushing the bank. Mairesse then repeatedly broke the lap record in regaining his second place. Schlesser was second until then.

Clark's Aston Martin was third, and Salvadori was delayed when a wheel collapsed. Beurly crashed his Ferrari, but without injury to himself.

Trintignant's Ferrari retired with gearbox trouble, and the Dick Stoop/Peter Riley Porsche Carrera lost time due to a tyre burst caused by pieces of the Beurly Ferrari littering the road. The Mason/Jaeger DB-Panhard was wrecked, but again the driver was only slightly hurt. Although the big cars had to stop two or three times for fuel, their tyres lasted out the race, humoured by the wet track.

Von Trips did a lap in 2min 58.5sec, equal to a speed of 97.64mph, but the Clark/Maggs Aston Martin broke a piston due to a valve sticking open after the engine had been stopped for re-fuelling. So, although the Ferraris truly dominated the 1000- kilometres, the finish was still exciting because Gendebien came in for a few gallons of fuel, just to make sure, and all the while Mairesse was going flat out in an effort to catch him.

The final result of this close-fought 1000-kilometre de Paris GT race was:

1st	0 Gendebien/L Bianchi (Ferrari) 624.591 miles, 90.346mph	
2nd	W Mairesse/W von Trips (Ferrari) 624.590 miles	
3rd	J Schlesser/A Simon (Ferrari) 614.903 miles	
4th	P Loustel/P Tavano (Ferrari) 600.346 miles	
5th	G Whitehead/H Taylor (Ferrari) 590.701 miles	
6th	R Salvadori/I lreland (Aston Martin) 585.862 miles	

Index of performance	B Consten/P Condriller (Abarth)
700-1000cc Class	R Boucharde/J Vidilles (DB)
1001-1600cc Class	G Hill/H von Hanstein (Porsche)
Over 1600cc Class	0 Gendebien/L. Bianchi (Ferrari)

This race injected fresh life into Montlhéry Autodrome as a race track.

The memorial to Antonio Ascari, killed in the 1925 French Grand Prix. (Denis Jenkinson)

The plaque to Alexandre Lamblin, creator of the Autodrome, on the front of the grandstand opposite the pits. (Denis Jenkinson)

A
Alexandre LAMBLIN
CREATEUR
de l'AUTODROME (1924)
Ses amis de l'automobile

Chapter 18

Two leading personalities

Many famous motor racing personalities have made history at
Montlhéry track, but two stand out, in my opinion, above all
others. I refer to Gwenda Stewart and Captain George Eyston.

Gwenda Stewart — quiet, tough, almost masculine in her love
of driving fast cars — could easily have been talented in other less-
exacting walks of life. Her father was Major-General Sir Frederick
Manley Glubb, CB, KCMG, DSO, who achieved great distinction
in the South African and First World Wars. Gwenda's brother was
Glubb Pasha, of the Arab Legion.

So, with this pedigree, it is not surprising that Gwenda Glubb
should wish to take an active, dangerous part in the Kaiser's war,
which resulted in her serving as an ambulance driver on the
Russian and Rumanian fronts. For her services she was awarded
the Crosses of St George and St Stanislaus, was mentioned in
despatches, and awarded British campaign medals.

After the war was over, Gwenda sought adventure in civilian
life — and found it by riding motorcycles in record attempts and
endurance runs. She began by riding a Ner-a-Car for 1000 miles
in daily stints of 190 mlles under ACU official observation, during
the severe winter of 1921.

In 1922 she attempted to break a double twelve-hour record at
Brooklands with a 249cc Trump-JAP, averaging 44.65mph.

At this period of her life Gwenda was associated with Lieut-Col
Stewart, whom she married. When Montlhéry opened she partnered
Colonel Stewart in further long distance motorcycle record
attempts, riding Rudge, Terrot-JAP and other fast machines.

The Stewarts found that they preferred to live in France, and
linked up with Douglas Hawkes who had a controlling interest

in the Derby Company just outside Paris. Douglas Hawkes had been intimately associated with motor racing for many years, prominent at Brooklands immediately after the war with cars ranging from Morgan three-wheelers to a giant 1912 15-litre Grand Prix Lorraine-Dietrich.

At Brooklands the Stewarts had operated the Brooklands Engineering Company, one of whose pursuits was to tune Rudge-Whitworth motorcycles, which they collected from the station at Weybridge and rode on the track at speeds for which Brooklands Certifcates were issued. After Montlhéry had opened, Gwenda Stewart and Douglas Hawkes transferred their interests to the French track, taking workshops under the curve of the home banking. From this depôt they concentrated on challenging records of every conceivable description, on motorcycles, in three-wheelers, cyclecars and cars. Eventually, Gwenda and Hawkes became man and wife.

I recently had the pleasure of chatting to Fred Cann about those days. Cann's father was well known as custodian of the gates at Brooklands (now installed at Goodwood), which led from the paddock onto the track itself, and through which every driver and car passed *en route* to success or failure.

Fred Cann joined Colonel Stewart at Brooklands in 1924, immediately after leaving school. In the winter of 1929-30 he was asked to go to Montlhéry to help Gwenda Stewart's Belgian mechanic prepare her record-breaking machines and, after recovering from appendicitis, he went out in January 1930. Soon, Cann was solely responsible for this exacting and arduous work, often being left alone by Douglas Hawkes for days on end preparing whichever car Gwenda was to drive next. He worked on her Morgans, standing by to change engines between record attempts, first in one class, then in another, besides supervising the runs; this, after having toiled for long hours preparing the cars. In the end Gwenda clocked 118mph at Arpajon in a specially narrow single-seater Morgan, an all-time three-wheeler record.

Perhaps the most important car Cann prepared was the

straight-eight, twin-overhead camshaft Derby-Miller. Hawkes had brought this 1½-litre front-wheel-drive Miller from America in 1930, with an American mechanic who was supposed to look after it. This man did not prove particularly useful, and soon Cann was in sole charge of this very fast racing car. (It was claimed to have achieved a speed of 139mph on the Altoona Speedway.)

No doubt Hawkes had been attracted by the very high speeds of which these centrifugally-supercharged cars were capable, while at the same time recognising that records achieved with a front-wheel-drive car would be good publicity for Derbys, also front-wheel driven.

Unfortunately, Fred Cann has lost the notebooks he compiled while working on the Derby-Miller, and, quite rightly, he refuses to rely on his memory; it being some quarter of a century since he last stripped the engine and took power output readings. However, as early as 1931, the engine was claimed to develop about 2bhp at 6500rpm, and later it was, as has been seen, developed to run much faster than that. At this time the straight-eight, five-bearing engine was quoted as measuring 59 x 76.5mm (1673cc), and used compression ratios varying from 6.8:1 to 8:1, depending on the duration of the records to be attempted. Blower pressure likewise varied, between 15 and 25psi. Martlett pistons, a speciality of the Brooklands Engineering Company, were used. The steel connecting rods were tubular, ignition was by Bosch magneto, and, in those days, a modified Wingfield downdraught carburetter was employed.

Frank Lockhart had achieved 164mph in the 1½-litre class with another Miller, so Hawkes decided to increase engine capacity and concentrate on record activities in Class E. The modifications deemed desirable increased the car's weight by three cwt. The alloy crankcase of the Miller engine was a cobweb-like structure; what with a full-length plate enclosing the base, big inspection plates on the side, and the openings for the two cylinder blocks on top. Given a few mechanical disasters such as broken pistons and connecting rods, little was left of the original.

Consequently, using the resources of the Derby factory, Hawkes cast new blocks and crankcase, at the same time converting the engine from American to metric studs and nuts. The de Dion-type front drive relied on a hollow axle tube which tended to distort, permitting the front wheels to assume odd angles, so Cann fitted two cross-bars between the spring hangers.

It was not long before all of the engine internals, and many of the chassis parts, owed more to Derby than Miller. For instance, two new centrifugal blowers were made in Paris. These ran at 40,000rpm as they were geared at five times crankshaft speed and, by now, the 1.6-litre engine was capable of a sustained 8000rpm.

The Miller had an unusual clutch which, when the pedal was right home, took the drive through a locklng pin. As engine power increased this pin used to shear, which Cann rectifed by using three ⁷⁄₁₆in pins. Eventually the car was justifiably known as the Derby Special, and Cann recalls that about the only Miller components remaining on it were the radiator shell and the Stromberg carburetter.

A second water header tank was fitted at the base of the radiator, connected to the normal header tank by vertical tubes passing through the gearbox; water leaks here being eliminated — after much trouble and strife — by fitting rubber grommets.

The engine was run on wood alcohol fuel after being started on benzole, and was lubricated with medicinal castor oil from a tank holding about eight gallons. This oil became very thin when hot, and the normal gear-type scavenge pump of the dry-sump lubrication system was unable to cope, so Cann fitted an extra pump driven by a small wooden propeller which once drove a fuel pump on an ancient aeroplane. This was located in front of the car's radiator. Normally, a rod protruding through the radiator grille held the propeller stationary, but when Gwenda saw that the oil temperature was around 85°C, she could pull back this rod, enabling the propeller to rotate in the air stream and drive the pump to supplement the main scavenge qump.

By the time Derby connecting rods, pistons and valves were in use, the car was not only extremely fast but reasonably reliable. Short plug life was the weakest feature of the engine, which caused attempts on the hour record to end in disappointment. The Derby Special always ran on Dunlop thin-tread tyres.

With the car, as recounted in earlier pages, Gwenda Stewart broke many records and finally lapped Montlhéry at fractionally under 149mph. In 1931 she had appeared, unsuccessfully, at Brooklands with the Derby-Miller. She brought the Derby Special to Brooklands again in 1935 for a match against Mrs Kay Petre's 10½-litre vee-twelve Delage. After preliminary troubles Gwenda broke the Brooklands Ladies' lap record with a speed of 135.95mph, which was never beaten. But the silencer – compulsory on the Brooklands track, did not suit the highly-tuned Derby engine. It is not generally known that, to assess the effect of this silencer on the plugs, a number of laps were covered in practice with an open exhaust, while Percy Bradley, Clerk of the Course, conveniently turned a blind eye, or should I say a deaf ear? Neither was the suspension suitable for high speed in what was still a very lightweight car, because the surface of Brooklands was far rougher than that of Montlhéry.

Gwenda was a fearless driver, modest and very quick to grasp mechanical matters, although confining her interest to driving the cars Hawkes and Cann prepared for her. At their bidding she would cut the ignition of the Derby at full throttle, using a button-switch on the steering wheel, so that they could 'read' the plugs after the car had stopped. It was through taking a hand from the wheel to poke the gear lever into neutral after making the customary ignition cut that Gwenda crashed badly after breaking the Montlhéry lap record; which means she had had the courage to throw out the clutch when travelling at a speed probably in excess of 150mph.

Although the Stewarts were denizens of Montlhéry, and invariably made their record bids with no-one present apart from the official observers and time-keepers, and perhaps a few personal friends, Gwenda Stewart always insisted that her car should be in complete and clean condition, and pushed out onto the track half an hour before a run was due to commence, and that her two mechanics should present themselves in spotless white overalls, which she supplied and paid the laundry bills for.

At Le Mans in 1934 Gwenda drove in the famous twenty-four-hour race with a sports front-wheel-drive Derby, and in 1935 Douglas Hawkes built a special 1½-litre Derby-Maserati for her to drive in road races. (This car appears today in events in England for historic racing cars.) Her main interest, however, continued to be track record-breaking.

Before the war the Hawkes returned to England to look after the greatly expanded Brooklands Engineering Company Ltd, which was housed in the one-time LBB shed in Brooklands paddock. This company specialized in supplying pistons and valves to the motor trade, as it continues to do very successfully today from a factory in Cobham. On the outbreak of the Second World War, the Hawkes' went over to the manufacture of munitions. One day, Gwenda approached Fred Cann, who was in charge of the factory, and said she was the only person in the place not fully helping the war effort. 'What can I do?' asked the famous lady racing driver. Soon, after a little instruction, she was one of Cann's best lathe operatives ...

Today, Gwenda and Douglas Hawkes sail the Mediterranean in their yacht *Eljois*. And Fred Cann? He lives where he was born; very close to what is left of Brooklands Track. He is not, unfortunately, very fit, but is as enthusiastic as ever and very willing to talk about the old days of motor racing at Weybridge and Montlhéry.

After Gwenda Hawkes, the British driver who made the greatest use of Montlhéry Track was probably Captain George Eyston, OBE, MC, who can be described as a professional record-breaker, as well as a qualified engineer. E A D Eldridge had discovered the value of Montlhéry — which was faster than Brooklands, although more tiring to negotiate at high speeds for record attempts — and was joined by Eyston for some of these onslaughts; Eyston can be said to have carried on where the late Ernest Eldridge left off.

Eyston was born on 20 June, 1897 at the Manor House, Bampton, Oxfordshire, not far from where, in later years, the MG Car Company supplied him with some of his finest record-breaking motorcars. His family had been known for hundreds of years in the Berkshire countryside, having its seat at East Hendred, where, for years, the old manor house retained a chapel saved during the Reformation.

Eyston was destined for an adventurous career. At Bampton he contrived to overturn an oil lamp in the nursery before he was a year old, the resultant fire of memorable proportions. As he grew up he concentrated on slightly safer pursuits, such as sailing his own boat, hunting and fishing, mainly in Ireland and the Outer Hebrides, and took easily to private flying when not being educated in the arts at Stonyhurst.

In what remained of his holidays, Eyston worked with a firm of marine engineers in Southampton, and found time to conduct some of the earliest air-to-ground wireless experiments, flying an aeroplane he had himself prepared for this research.

All this occupied George before August 1914; when war was declared he enlisted in the Public Schools and Universities Battalion as a private.

Eyston received a commission in the Dorsets, and later transferred to the Royal Field Artillery. He went out to France early in 1915, subsequently becoming ADC to General Wellesley, commanding the 21st Divisional Royal Artillery.

He was wounded in May 1917 but went back to France to serve on the Staff until the end of the war. Captain G E T Eyston was mentioned in despatches and was awarded the Military Cross.

In January 1919 he went up to Trinity College, Cambridge, where he was a fellow-undergraduate of Prince Albert (later King George VI) and the Duke of Gloucester. He not only studied engineering with distinction, but was Captain of the First Trinity Boat Club and spare man to the Cambridge crew which won the international Eights on the River Seine in 1919.

After leaving Cambridge, Eyston joined the Marine Department of J Stone & Co, and subsequently became a member of John I Thornycroft & Co Ltd, and a Director of Jarvis & Sons of Wimbledon.

After witnessing the French Grand Prix of 1921, to which he drove in his GN, Eyston turned to motor racing, at first as an additional relaxation, racing Aston Martin and Grand Prix Bugatti cars at Brooklands and in road races. He married in 1923 and has two daughters, Magdalen and Betty.

George soon turned his engineering knowledge to the development of the Powerplus supercharger, and to preparing cars for innumerable record attempts and a certain amount of racing, driving them himself. His many successes and few failures, not to mention narrow escapes, in this exacting field are described in my history of Brooklands Track and in the foregoing pages.

Later, Eyston tried his hand at attempts on world records in Utah, and chalked up some notable figures with his special car *Speed of the Wind*. He twice held the world Land Speed Record with his fabulous eight-wheeled, 5000hp, six-ton *Thunderbolt* at the wheel of which, in 1939, he covered the two-way mile at a speed of 357.5mph; a record beaten, even today, only by the late John Cobb. George has kindly written the Preface to this book.

Chapter 19

An update

Without the glory of the French Grands Prix races, for which the Montlhéry road circuit was well suited, by the 1960s the world impact of the French Autodrome was somewhat diminished. Some of the former regular events were continued for some years, but, in general, later races there were of rather more minor interest, just as our Brooklands meetings, whilst enormously popular here, were practically unheard of abroad, except by avid motor racing followers.

It was record-breaking in all classes and categories which continued as the major pursuit at the banked French circuit, with the important advantage of Montlhéry being available for round-the-clock use, unlike the ban on night-time running on Brooklands Track to humour the demands of noise-objecting local residents. John Cobb and other drivers agreed that the more steeply banked French track was also smoother than its British counterpart, but also more tiring to drive on for long periods because its straights were shorter. At Brooklands the half-mile of the Railway straight allowed a driver to relax to some extent, although negotiation of the Vickers reverse curve in the faster cars required concentration.

In 1961 the former fixtures pattern was followed at Montlhéry for some time. The Prix de Paris was held that May, in two heats. The winner was Boyer in a Lotus-Ford, followed by the DB-Panhard driven by Boucharde and the Lotus-Ford of Piper. Another of these races, held in September, was won by Siffert's Lotus-Ford, followed by another of these cars in the hands of Grandsire, with third place occupied by Rosinsky driving a Cooper-BMC. These contests between the Formula Junior cars were wound up with the 140km

Coupe du Salon race won by Love and Maggs, both with Cooper-BMCs, who tied after a battle lasting for just over one hour and seven minutes.

The 1961 sports car Gran Turismo races comprised two more Coupe de Paris events and a 70km Coupe du Salon. The first of these was a victory for Simon's 250GT Ferrari from the Porsches of Fraissinet and Monneret; the winner's speed 120.264kph. The second went to Oreiller (Ferrari 250GT) at 119.944kph (74.53mph), followed by Monneret (Porsche) and Schlesser (Ferrari 250GT). The Coupe du Salon event was won by Oreiller (Ferrari 250GT), with 'Remordu' (Ferrari 250GT) second and Koch (Porsche Abarth) in third place. The Paris 1000km was a walkover for the Ferrari 250GTs of the Rodriguez brothers, Mairesse/Bianchi, and Trintignant/Vaccarella, a race won at an average speed of 153.596kph (95.44mph).

Much the same programme was followed for the 1962 season. It opened with the Spring Cup race which held interest for British enthusiasts because it was won by a Brabham-Ford driven by Schlesser, another car of the same kind second, with Moench as its occupant, and third place taken by Francis' Caravelle-Ford – the winning speed 126.340kph (78.50mph). In April the USA Cup was a victory for Berney (Ferrari 250GT), followed by Spinedi in another Ferrari 250GT, and the AC-Bristol of Magne third. This was followed in May with the Paris Cup event, another success for the Spring Cup victor, who was followed home by the Cooper-BMCs of Boucharde and Cowles.

The second Paris Cup assignment was a 1-2-3 for Boucharde, Hitches, and Periat respectively in Cooper-BMC, Lola-Ford and another Cooper-BMC, the speed of the winner for the 77km being 117.695kph (73.13mph). In September the Paris Cup was won by Laureau (Rene Bonnet), at a speed of 122.901kph (76.37mph), with Koch (Porsche-Abarth) and Morand (Lotus Elite) in second and third places. One Salon Cup contest saw a triple finish for the Lotus-Fords of Arundell, Anderson and Grandsire, Arundell's speed 131.287kph (81.58mph), and the other a triple finish for

Ferrari GTOs driven by Berney, Simon and Remordu; the winning speed was 130.992kph (81.40mph).

The season was wound-up in October with the 1000km of Paris race for GT cars of all classes, which was decided after a long battle of the Ferrari GTOs. In the end the Ferrari of the Rodriguez brothers took the flag after averaging 157.736kph (98mph), a matter of a combined driving spell lasting for over six hours and 21 minutes. Second place went to the Ferrari shared by John Surtees and Mike Parkes, with third place occupied by Colin Davis and Scarfiotti. The fastest lap had been made by Willie Maresse's Ferrari in two minutes and 52.2 seconds. The finishers were another Ferrari GTO, two Porsche Carrera-Abarths and an Abarth-Simca, the Lotus-Elite of Wagstaff and Baird, and a Lotus-Ford 23. In practice French driver Paul Armagnac crashed and was fatally injured.

The programme for 1963 was almost identical to the earlier annual programme, the Prix de Paris races in two heats being won by Frank Gardener's Brabham-Ford from Schlesser's Brabham-Ford and Revson's Cooper-Ford. Schlesser's Brabham-Ford won the only Coupe du Salon, at 122.340kph (76mph) from Offenstadt's Lola-Ford and Martel's Brabham-Ford. A 57km Prix de Paris was won by the Lotus 23 of Beckwith from Hegbourne's sister car and Vogele's Lotus-Climax. The 60km Salon Cup contest went to Schlesser, now driving an Aston Martin GT4, at 117.821kph (73.21mph), second place with taken by Guichet's Ferrari GTO, and third by Richard's Abarth-Simca.

In 1964 the shorter races commenced in May with the 67.5km Coupe de Paris event for Grand Touring Cars. The winner was Sutcliffe, in a Jaguar E-type which did 132.211kph (82.15mph). Koch's Porsche 904 was second and Ligier's car of this type took third place. Next, also in May, came the Coupe de Paris in the customary couple of heats form, confined to Formula 3 cars, of which Bianchi's Alpine-Renault came in first. The next two to finish were Englishman Crichton-Stuart in a Cooper-BMC and Jean Behra driving a Lotus-Ford.

The closing part of the year witnessed the Ille de France 117km race which Grandsire's Alpine-Renault won at 145.139kph (90.19mph), from Chambers' Brabham-Ford and the Cooper-BMC of Jaussaud. In September Montlhéry defied the weather with another Ille de France engagement, this time over 249km, won by the Brabham-Cosworth of (Sir) Jack Brabham with (Sir) Jackie Stewart's Lotus-Cosworth second, and third position occupied by Schlesser in another Brabham-Cosworth; the winner's speed 158.504kph (98.49mph). Soon afterwards there was the 16-lap Coupe du Salon, Jackie Stewart taking the victor's prize in a Lotus-Cortina in this touring car dice, from Sir J Whitmore's Lotus-Cortina and Issermann's Alfa-Romeo TI, Stewart averaging 122.192kph (75.93mph). That day also, an 80km Coupe du Salon race went to Offenstadt's Cooper-Ford at 130.948kph from Stiller's Lotus-Ford and Irwin's Merlyn-Ford. The day's racing included another Coupe du Salon, this time contested over 20 laps of the road course, and won by Patria's Abarth-Simca from Steinmetz in another Abarth-Simca, and Garant's Ferrari GTO, at a speed of 127.769kph (79.39mph).

This was a year when Montlhéry was very much in Britain's favour, with the top fixture of the Paris 1000km being won by Graham Hill/Bonnier at 153.518kph (95.39mph), from Rodriguez/Schlesser's Ferrari GTO and the Porsche 904/8 of Barth and Colin Davis, son of Sammy Davis. Due to an accident in which two drivers and three officials were killed, this fixture was not held in 1965 though was resumed for 1966.

The pattern was almost the same in 1965. Beckwith won two of the Paris Cup races. The first was over 66.4km, which he won at 131.707kph (81.84mph) from Fraissinet's Lotus 23-Ford and Wingfield's Crossie. The second of these races, over 15 laps, saw the three first places filled by Lotus Elans, Beckwith winning at 127.433kph (79.19mph) from Dauwe and Humberset. Crichton-Stuart's Brabham-Ford scored in the 83km Paris Cup event, which he won at 123.117kph (76.50mph) from Stiller's Lotus-Ford and Williams' Brabham-Ford, and he took the 80km Coupe du Salon event in a Brabham-Ford at 131.046kph (81.43mph), followed by Beltoise in a Matra-Ford and Weber's Alpine-Renault. The 67km Coupe du Salon was won by Ruata's Abarth 2000 at 129.186kph (80.27mph). He was followed home by the Porsche 904 GTs of Bechet and Meert.

There was more activity in 1966, with two Ille de France events, the winner of the 257km race Jack Brabham's Brabham-Honda, at 162.231kph (100.81mph), from Clark's Lotus-Cosworth and Hulme's Brabham-Honda; the other was won by Weber (Alpine-Renault) at 151.084kph (93.88mph), followed by the Lotus-Fords of Cardwell and Hart. The Coupe du Salon was won by Jaussaud's Matra-Ford, and the two heats of the Paris Cup both won by Revson (Lotus-Ford). A second Coupe du Salon was won by Ortner's Abarth 2000. There was also the 67km Paris race, which was a triple finish of Porsche Carrera 6s led by that of van Lennap. The resumed 1000km race was a victory for Piper/Parkes in a Ferrari 275LM.

This event in 1967 was won by Ickx and Hawkins, whose Ford-Mirage beat a Ferrari 330P and a Porsche. The Paris Cup for Formula Three cars was taken by Depailler's Alpine-Renault and the two Coupe du Salon by Pilette's Alfa-Romeo GTA and Vidal's Matra-Ford. An additional event – the 50km Group 6 sports car contest – was won by Pescarolo's Matra-Ford V8.

Well-established races were continued season after season. Thus, in 1968, there were two Prix de Paris events; that in the Formula Three category won by Cevert's Tecno-Ford, and the one for sportscars by Gavin's Matra-Ford V8, with Dal Bo's Pygmee-Ford taking the only Coupe du Salon. The Paris Cup and the Coupe de Vitesse were won by Jabouille in a Matra-Ford, and the Paris 1000km by Herrmann/Stommelen (Porsche 908).

The following year's racing was much the same as before. The Formula Three Prix de Paris in the two heats was again a tie, this time between Schenken and Wisell in Brabham-Ford and Chevron-Ford cars. Fittipaldi's Lotus-Ford took the Coupe du Salon. The 67.4km Prix de Paris was a first for Joe Bonnier's Lola-

Chevrolet V8, but it was the similarly named race over 1000km that was the great attraction, both for entrants and spectators. It was won at 169.707kph (105.45mph) by the Matra 650 driven by Beltoise and Pescarola, second place taken by Rodriguez and Redman in a Matra 630/650, with third place occupied by Piper and Craft driving a Porsche 908. It was Piper who won the Coupe de Vitesse sports car event in a Lola-Chevrolet V8 and Martin's Ford GT40 that took the second of these races.

So, the racing at Montlhéry continued, spectators able to drive there the short distance from Paris, and some, perhaps, along the famous Arpajon road where speed trials had been held and on which Ernest Eldridge, in the monster Fiat, had bravely broken the Land Speed Record in 1924. The usual programme of races was maintained in 1970; the Coupe de Vitesse being won by Jaussaud's Tecno-Ford and the two Coupe du Salons by Fittipaldi's Lotus-Ford and Larrousse in a Porsche 908. Beuttler's Brabham-Ford secured victory in the Paris Grand Prix, and a new fixture — the AGACI race — saw Ligier's Ligier JS1 take first place, as did Attwood in another innovation, the Spring Cup, with a Lola-Chevrolet-V8. All was overshadowed by the 1000km marathon, in which Brabham and Cever in a Matra-Simca 660 took the honours, at a speed of 171.763kph (106.73mph).

There was a noticeable diminution in top racing activity at Montlhéry in 1971; the situation was the same in 1972, and it was closed temporarily in 1973. It was still intact in 2000 and was remembered for some time by French enthusiasts and those from Britain, especially by members of the Vintage Sports Car Club and the Morgan Three-Wheeler Club, when members took their cars and motorcycles to the Montlhéry events organised by the late Jacques Protherow, after which the place finally closed completely and became out-of-bounds.

The existing state of Montlhéry is well-described and illustrated in *Autodrome — the lost race circuits of Europe* by S S Collins and Gavin J Ireland (Veloce Publishing Ltd), which describes their visits to some of these forgotten European race circuits.

Index

225

Index

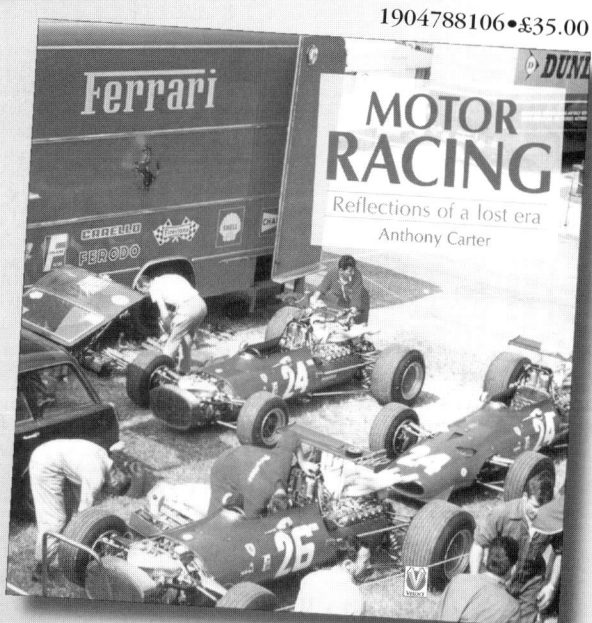

1845840372•£17.99

1904788157•29.99